LAST OF THE
ROBBERS
ROOST
OUTLAWS

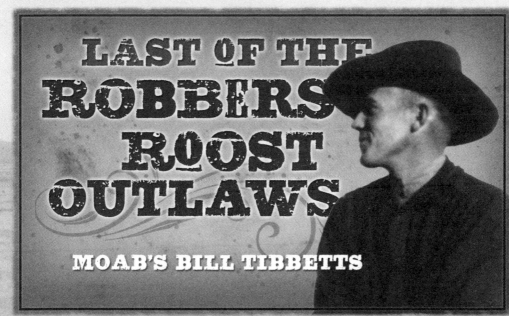

LAST OF THE ROBBERS ROOST OUTLAWS

MOAB'S BILL TIBBETTS

by Tom McCourt

CANYONLANDS
Natural History Association

Composed and printed in the United States of America

Design by David Jenney
Edited by Elizabeth A. Green and Karla Hancock
FIRST IMPRESSION 2010
ISBN 978-0-937407-15-8

14   5

To Ray Tibbetts
A good man and a chip off the old block

CONTENTS

LABYRINTH CANYON

HORSESHOE CANYON

MINERAL CANYON

HORSETHIEF POINT

NORTH

5 KILOMETERS
5 MILES

MOAB

191

313

128

279

191

BIG FLAT

HORSETHIEF CANYON

GOOSENECK

DEAD HORSE POINT

COLORADO RIVER

GREEN RIVER

WHITE RIM

ISLAND IN THE SKY

ROBBERS ROOST AREA

QUEEN ANNS BOTTOM

ANDERSON BOTTOM

TURKS HEAD

WHITE RIM

MEANDER CANYON

STILLWATER CANYON

GRAND VIEW POINT

WHITE RIM

GREEN RIVER

RIVER

COLORADO

ORANGE CLIFFS

ELATERITE BASIN

THE MAZE

THE CONFLUENCE

CANYONLANDS NATIONAL PARK

COLORADO RIVER

CATARACT CANYON

THE NEEDLES

211

AUTHOR'S NOTE

MUCH OF THIS STORY TAKES PLACE IN WHAT IS KNOWN TODAY AS CANYONLANDS NATIONAL PARK. The map and descriptions will help the reader better understand some of the geography, place names, and locations.

Island in the Sky is a high mesa, between the rivers, near the confluence of the Green and Colorado rivers. Today it is in the northern end of Canyonlands National Park. Early cowboys called it an "island" because it has vertical sandstone walls on all four sides, and is separated from the rest of the world by a narrow neck of land, just wide enough for a road. The road connects the island with the Big Flat country to the north. From the river canyons, more than 2000 feet below, the top of the mesa appears to be touching the clouds, hence the name, Island in the Sky. At the southern tip of the island is Grandview Point, one of the most impressive overlooks in all of Canyonlands National Park.

The White Rim is a wide sandstone shelf below Island in the Sky. In elevation, it is halfway between the top of Island in the Sky and the Green and Colorado rivers. The White Rim is named for a distinctive layer of hard white sandstone that is exposed at the outer edge of the formation. The White Rim can be seen clearly from places like Grandview Point.

Key players in this story and their cattle brands

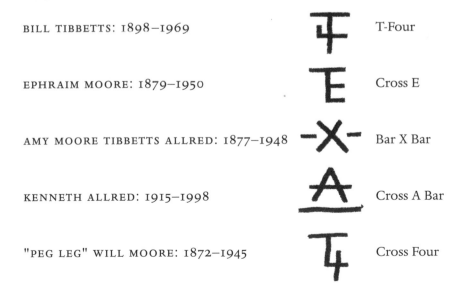

BILL TIBBETTS: 1898–1969 — T-Four

EPHRAIM MOORE: 1879–1950 — Cross E

AMY MOORE TIBBETTS ALLRED: 1877–1948 — Bar X Bar

KENNETH ALLRED: 1915–1998 — Cross A Bar

"PEG LEG" WILL MOORE: 1872–1945 — Cross Four

Bill Tibbetts, 1947

INTRODUCTION

THIS BOOK TELLS A TRUE STORY. JAMES WILLIAM (Bill) Tibbetts, Jr. was a real man, a real cowboy, and a real outlaw. And he really was the last of the Robbers Roost outlaws. He was also a good man by most accounts, a devoted family man who loved his wife and children and took care of his twice-widowed mother. Even some of his strongest enemies came to like him and call him friend. Few people have ever heard his name and only a handful have ever known his story, until now. It is a fascinating tale, beyond fiction and imagination.

This story is written through the perspective of the Tibbetts family. It is taken from family records and accounts written by Bill's relatives, children, and friends. There is a rich oral history in the family, too, accounts of things Bill said and did while interacting with his family and the community of Moab, Utah.

Most of this story is in the public record. Early newspaper accounts have many references of Bill Tibbetts, and most are used in their entirety in this book, even though the news stories don't always tell the same story Bill told his children. There are other first-person accounts besides Bill's that cast doubt on some of the things reported in the newspapers, too. News reporting has always been inexact, and that was especially true in the early 1900s when news and editorial opinion were often intertwined. For the purposes of this book, the author follows the Tibbetts family account while using the newspaper stories for backdrop, contrast, and a taste of the times. The newspaper stories have been copied with the actual spelling, punctuation, and sentence structure intact as much as possible.

Some references and dialogue in this book are regional colloquialisms that were in common use at the time of the story. For example, the term "cedars" was often used to describe pinyon and juniper trees. The word "desert" can mean anywhere in southern Utah. The term "Book Cliffs" can mean all of the land north of Interstate 70.

The author has also included the stories of the last two "Indian wars" in San Juan County. Not because this story is about Indians, but because the tragic events leading to, and culminating in, brutality and injustice toward the Native Americans fits hand-in-glove with the Bill Tibbetts story. The Indian stories and the Bill Tibbetts story were parallel events, happening at the same time, in the same general area, and with essentially the same cast of characters. The Indian stories speak volumes about the mindset, passions, and prejudices of the times.

In telling the Indian stories, the author has, with sarcasm, used a few of the prejudiced racial terms used in the newspapers and other accounts at the time. Wherever these terms are used, they have been placed in quotation marks to indicate they are quotes or colloquial slang, such as "squaws, bucks, and papooses," and "war-painted savages." Certainly, no offense is intended in referencing these archaic and distasteful terms. They simply help to paint the story in its original colors.

All dialogue in this book is purely fictional. It is used only to set the stage and as a means to explain and expound on certain topics and events. All place names are real. The names of the characters are real, too.

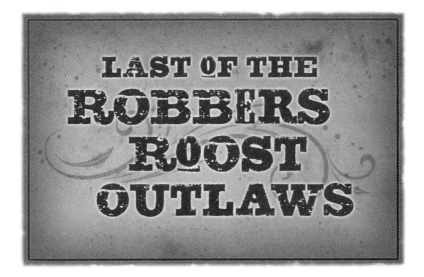

Amy Moore Tibbetts and brother Ephriam

CHAPTER I

THE BIRTH OF A LEGEND

IN THE 1890S, UTAH'S SAN JUAN COUNTY was still a blank spot on most maps. The area was one of the last frontiers in the continental United States, a vast region of tangled red rock canyons, cedar mesas, and dusty-blue sagebrush flats. Roads were primitive, distances were long, and the westerly wind swept wild and free across millions of acres of empty sage and canyon country.

On the south side of the La Sal mountain range, a few pioneer farms and ranches were scattered through the sage and oak brush. There was no town there in the true sense of the word, only a general store with a few outbuildings, but the site was called La Sal. In later years, it would be known as old La Sal.

It was a land of many perils. Lawmen, clergymen, doctors, merchants, and neighbors were often hard to find. Pioneer families dealt with sickness, accidents, birth, death, and bad men as best they could.

It was a cold afternoon when eighteen-year-old Ephraim Moore came down the muddy wagon road toward old La Sal. The tops of the mountains were still wrapped in snow and a forest of oak brush spread leafless and barren across miles of rolling foothills and up the mountainsides. A blue winter's haze hung heavy in the air, filtering the sunshine like fine indigo silk.

The young man was sitting high on the buckboard wrapped in an old wool coat with a wide-brimmed hat pulled low over his eyes. The horses sloshed through the sticky mud with shoulders tight against the harness, the wagon following obediently while rocking like a ship on the uneven roadway. The boy mumbled a popular song of the day, low and to himself, into the collar of his coat and under his breath. From a few feet away his off-key efforts sounded more like a moan of pain than any song another person might have recognized.

Young Ephraim was on his way to visit the wilderness homestead of his older sister, Amy Moore Tibbetts, and her new husband, Bill. He had been traveling all day over the rocks and ruts of the pioneer wagon track and he was tired, hungry, and eager to have his journey done. His feet were braced against the splashboard to help cushion the jarring punishment of the hardboard spring seat and his fingers were numb from holding the reins for hours in the cold, high desert air. The horses plodded along wearily with heads down and legs covered with mud to their knees. The wagon squeaked and rattled.

The weary horses finally topped a long rise and the young man could see his destination. The little cabin nestled snug against the shelter of a wooded ridge with pole fences and corrals spread wide across the frozen meadow. It was a welcoming sight with the early shadows of evening beginning to creep across the valley.

The homestead presented a scene of peace and tranquility, but as Ephraim got closer, he could sense that something wasn't right. Before he reached the yard he could hear livestock in the corral bawling to be fed, and the big dog that ran out to greet him seemed tense and agitated. He noticed that the cow hadn't been milked that afternoon and there was no smoke from the chimney of the cabin. The March weather was much too cold not to have a fire.

Ephraim pulled the wagon up near the cabin and climbed down. From the look of things, no one was at home, and it didn't appear that anyone had been there all day. The boy was concerned about that. He'd been sent by his mother to check on his sister who would soon deliver her first child. His instructions were to take her back to Moab where she could have the baby in the comfort of her mother's home with a proper midwife in attendance. But where could his sister be? Ephraim had traveled almost forty miles and he needed a place to spend the night.

The young man rapped on the cabin door, then pulled it open a crack and hollered cautiously, "Hello sister, it's Ephraim. Don't shoot me." Immediately there was a groan from the semi-darkness within the cabin, and then he heard his sister's tearful cry, "Ephraim! Oh, thank God! …I need some help, Eph. …I need some help."

Ephraim rushed into the cabin to find his sister lying on the bed covered with a bloodstained blanket. "The baby's coming, Eph. I need some help," she pleaded. She then slammed her teeth together on a corner of the blanket to suppress a wild animal scream.

"What are ya doin', Amy?" the boy muttered in complete shock and bewilderment. "That baby ain't due fer another month or more. You can't have it now, not here, not like this."

"You gotta get some help, Eph. Run to the Cross-H Ranch and get that lady who cooks down there. She knows me and she'll come."

"Where's Bill, Amy? Your husband ought ta be here."

"He's on the range with the cows," she groaned through clenched teeth. "Won't be back until tomorrow. Go get that woman at the Cross-H."

"Gawd, Amy, I can't leave you here like this. Not like this."

"Git!" she screamed with pain, impatience, and anger. "You go get that lady cook and don't you waste one minute!"

Ephraim charged from the cabin and vaulted to the wagon seat. He left the yard with the wagon wheels throwing mud and the horses' necks bowed under the threat of his stinging whip. The big dog ran alongside, yapping excitedly while chasing him down the muddy road. The Cross-H Ranch was two or three miles down the valley.

When Eph got to the ranch he found the lady cook was gone and wouldn't be back for a few more days. None of the cowboys was willing to volunteer for midwife duty. The young man was stuck. There was no doctor, no hospital, no midwife, no woman, no relative, and no friend to come to his aid and help him deliver his sister's baby. Panic overwhelmed him as the reality set in.

As the boy turned to go back to his sister's cabin with his heart in his throat, one of the cowboys handed him a doctor book. "The part about delivering babies is on page twenty-three. Good luck, kid."

That's how it happened. James William (Bill) Tibbetts, Jr. was born in that cold log cabin with his teenaged uncle, Ephraim Moore, acting as midwife. The date was March 23, 1898. It was the rough and tumble beginning of a remarkable life.

CHAPTER 2

A MURDER MOST FOUL

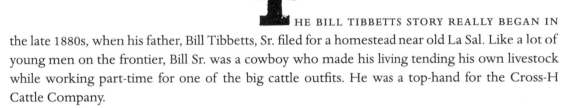

THE BILL TIBBETTS STORY REALLY BEGAN IN the late 1880s, when his father, Bill Tibbetts, Sr. filed for a homestead near old La Sal. Like a lot of young men on the frontier, Bill Sr. was a cowboy who made his living tending his own livestock while working part-time for one of the big cattle outfits. He was a top-hand for the Cross-H Cattle Company.

When the young man decided to build a ranch of his own, he picked a good location in the shadow of Pine Ridge, where a spring of cold water bubbled up from the oak brush. He made a fine two-room cabin there, with outbuildings, corrals, and pine pole fences. Bill was proud of his place, and he worked hard to build up a good herd of cattle.

Available women were in short supply on the Utah frontier, and Bill was approaching middle age and still single when he met and fell madly in love with Amy Moore, a teenaged girl from Moab who came to cook for the Cross-H Ranch. It was common in those days for older men to court and marry younger women, and the two of them hit it off very well. Amy was a pretty girl who had many suitors, but she was charmed by the handsome cowboy who owned his own spread and offered a ready-made cabin all furnished and waiting. They were married in 1897. He was forty and she was almost twenty when they began life together at the Tibbetts Ranch.

Amy Ellen Moore was the perfect wife for a frontier cowboy. She was strong, independent, and resourceful, the daughter of Mormon pioneers who had walked to Utah from Nauvoo, Illinois, pulling a handcart. She was no stranger to hard work and wilderness. Her parents, Joseph and Hannah Moore, had helped pioneer the settlements of Pleasant Grove, Utah, and Bennington and Fishhaven, Idaho. Then, in 1889, when Amy was twelve, the family moved to the red rock country of Moab and broke ground for a farm along the southern edge of the little community.

OPPOSITE: *Moab City, early 1900s*

Amy loved her husband. He was everything she ever wanted in a man. He was tall, handsome, and well mannered. He treated her with respect. He was considerate of her moods, mindful of her needs, and he loved the desert country the way she did. He promised her that just as soon as he could, he was going to build her a fine home of red desert sandstone, with bedrooms upstairs and white-painted porches. Their marriage was blessed with two sons: Bill Jr., born in the wilderness cabin in 1898, and Joe, who was born in Moab in November 1899.

———— · · ————

The sound of an ax echoed across the frozen meadow. It was the evening of March 19, 1902, and Bill Tibbetts, Sr. was chopping wood and stacking it against the side of the cabin. Tomorrow he would leave to spend a few days with his cattle and he wanted Amy to have a good supply of firewood. Household chores and little boys kept her very busy.

It was a pretty time of day. Shadows were growing long and the late afternoon sun lit the snowy tips of the mountains with a soft, orange sheen. Bill's little boys were playing in the dirt near the woodpile and Amy was peeling potatoes in the cabin.

The barking of the dog drew Bill's attention to a surrey coming down the muddy lane. He recognized the roan horse and the black-topped carriage as belonging to his old friend, Charlie Rose. Charlie might have been the oldest man in San Juan County, as far as Bill could tell. Old man Rose always told people that he was ninety, but he'd been saying that for years. The old man drove the buggy into the yard and Bill was shocked to see a very haggard and bloody young woman sitting next to him on the seat. Bill recognized the woman as the teenaged wife of Charles Bothe, a neighbor from up the valley. Charlie Bothe had a bad reputation. He was known to be a bully and a drunk.

"What's going on, Mr. Rose?" Bill asked as he walked up to the surrey, but he already knew the answer. Dutch Charlie, as the locals knew Bothe, had done this thing before. The man had a horrible temper. He was callous, cruel, and fond of the devil's brew. His young wife was a constant target of his drunken fury. He had beaten her terribly several times in recent months.

"Saw her hidin' in the oak bushes up on the hillside," old man Rose offered. "That red apron and bloody face gave her away. She ain't got no coat and she'll freeze fer shore if she stays out all night. I didn't know what to do with her, so I brought her to you. I figured maybe your missus could fix her up and get her somethin' to eat. She's been beat up somethin' awful."

Bill could see that both of the girl's eyes were black and her lip was split and badly swollen. Her dark hair was a tangled mess and there was blood on the front of her dress and apron. He tenderly extended a hand to help the girl down from the buggy. "Are you going to be all right, Mary?" he asked.

"Dutch Charlie'll kill us both if you help me, Mr. Tibbetts." The young woman sobbed. "He's really on one this time. He said he'd kill me if I ran away and he's out lookin' for me now. He's got a gun and he'll kill us both, for sure."

"Now, now, don't you worry about that," Bill assured her. "Old Charlie is drunk and he'll come around when he sobers up in the morning. You come in the house and let Amy take a look at that lip. We've got a place you can stay tonight and supper's almost ready."

Amy came from the cabin as Bill was helping the girl down from the surrey. She stopped in stunned silence and put her hand over her mouth in shock as she saw the damage done to the pretty young face. Tears came to her eyes and it took a moment to regain her composure. Then, taking a deep breath, she stepped forward and said, "You come inside, Mary. I've got hot water on the stove and we'll get washed up for supper."

As Amy helped the whimpering girl into the cabin, Bill turned to old man Rose. "You might as well stay tonight, too," he said. It's a long ways back to your place and you'll be travelin' in the dark before you get there. You might as well stay and make an early start in the morning."

"Thank you, Bill. I'll do that," the old man said. And then he turned and looked back up the road, the way he had come. "Old Dutch Charlie might be here in a little while. I'm sure he's out lookin' for her. You might want to load that 30-30 and keep it in yer hand."

"Ole Dutch Charlie doesn't scare me any," Bill said with real conviction. "I know the man pretty well. I've even hired him a couple of times. He's a holy terror to that little girl when he's drunk, but I've never seen him tangle with a full-grown man. I got no respect for a man like that. I wish he'd try me one time. I'd like to bust his face for all he's done to that little wife of his."

"Yeah, but it's a family matter," old man Rose said quietly. "Outsiders shouldn't get involved in family matters."

"Maybe so," Bill growled. "But that man is gonna kill that girl one of these days if someone doesn't get involved. She shouldn't have to take a beating like that for any reason. I'm gonna talk to the sheriff about it the first chance I get. Maybe the law can do somethin' about this."

———◦•◦———

The Tibbetts family and their invited guests had just settled down for their evening meal when the dog announced the approach of a stranger. The cabin was crowded and there weren't enough chairs. Bill put his plate down on the bed where he had been sitting and went for the door. As he passed the kitchen table he put his hand on old man Rose's shoulder and said, "You stay here. I'll take care of this."

It was getting dark outside, almost too dark to see, and quite cold, too. Bill closed the door behind him and stepped out into the yard. There, in the semi-darkness stood Dutch Charlie Bothe. The big man looked larger than life in his old buffalo robe coat that hung down past his knees. A floppy felt hat covered his head and the bottom of his face was hidden in a tangle of whiskers. A big 45-90 buffalo rifle was in his hand.

"I've come to take my woman home," the big man hissed. The smell of whiskey and vomit hung heavy in the air. The dog growled and Bill told it to shut up and lie down.

"She's stayin' here tonight," Bill told the man with more confidence than he felt. "You can come an get her tomorrow when you sober up some."

"By God, I'll take her now!" the drunkard growled.

"You take her now and I'll have you arrested," Bill promised. "I'll file a complaint with the county court and we'll have the sheriff here in no time at all. The way that girl is beat up, it'll cost you twenty dollars just to get out of jail."

"I ought ta blow your damn head off."

"You put that rifle down and let's see if you can knock my damn head off," Bill challenged. "I'll give you the first swing."

The big man mumbled an obscenity, but then turned on his heel and started back out into the night. As he stomped away, he called back over his shoulder, "I'll get you, Tibbetts, you dirty somnabitch." Bill took three or four steps toward the retreating drunk, but then thought better of it. No one had ever called him that before without losing some teeth, but the man was drunk and he was out there in the dark with a rifle. Bill decided to wait and settle with the bastard later.

Things quieted down around the cabin after that. Amy made beds for Mr. Rose and Mary Bothe. The little boys went to sleep in the crib and Amy was washing dishes. Bill sat at the kitchen table near a coal oil lamp, reading a two-week-old newspaper. His loaded 30-30 was standing in the corner.

———— · · ————

The blast blew window glass all over the room. There was a terrific flash of light, a horrendous noise, and blue smoke filled the cabin air. The women screamed, old man Rose stumbled toward the back of the cabin dressed only in his long underwear, and Bill Tibbetts slumped from his chair to the floor, his shirt soaked with blood. Bothe kicked the door open and

MARCH 28, 1902

The Grand Valley Times

MURDER MOST FOUL

Detailed information of the killing of Mrs. Mary Bothe and William Tibbetts at La Sal creek, last week points to but one conclusion that it was a case of murder most foul. Chas. Bothe the murdered was arrested at Paradox, Colo. and has been taken to the Montrose county jail to await the arrival of San Juan county officers. The story he tells as reported from that place, is to the effect that he was playing the role of the wronged husband seeking revenge.

The facts on the contrary show that his wife was at the Tibbetts ranch for food and shelter, and to escape the brutal condition he was surrounding her with. She was but about 17 years of age, and had been brought into that country by Bothe from her home at Leadville, had been left long distances from neighbors, without food or clothing. That she had left Bothe several times and sought shelter at neighbors, but Bothe would come and with threats of taking her life, compel her to return. Tibbetts had employed Bothe on his ranch in order that conditions would be better for the woman, but he had not remained. Sometime before the killing, Mr. Chas. Rose, who is stopping at the Tibbetts ranch, a man about 90 years of age, found Mrs. Bothe wandering in the brush and taken her to the ranch.

Bothe came to the ranch on the fatal evening while the men were at the supper table and accused Tibbetts of stealing his wife, she stepping in from another room spoke to him when cursing her he raised his rifle and shot her through the back. He then turned the rifle on Tibbetts who sought shelter in the pantry. Bothe breaking in the door shot him in the back. He then rides to a neighboring ranch and informs Mr. Lackey that old man Rose has been kicked by a horse and needs help, returning to the Tibbetts place he drags Tibbetts and Mrs. Bothe out to the light compels Mr. Rose to open their clothing as to see the wounds, expresses satisfaction that they will prove to be fatal, shakes hands with his victims and rides off.

dragged his screaming young wife out into the night. A moment later came a thundering shot and the screaming stopped. Amy ran to her terrified little boys and covered them with her body, sobbing uncontrollably. She had seen her husband fall and she knew he was dead.

Little Bill Tibbetts, Jr. was a few days short of his fourth birthday, but he never forgot the horror of that night. For the rest of his life he would mourn the loss of the father he never got to know; and he would often remember what a hero his mother was when she put her body between him and the bullets that never came.

APRIL 18, 1902

The Grand Valley Times

Judge McCarty, reporter Rollo, and District Attorney Livingston left last evening for Monticello to hold court. The preliminary hearing of Charles Bothe for the murder of his wife and William Tibbets will be held before Judge McCarty.

AUGUST 22, 1902

The Grand Valley Times

BOTHE FOUND GUILTY

Charles Bothe the man who is charged with the murder of his wife and Mr. Tibbetts last April was tried in the District Court at Monticello yesterday for the murder of Tibbetts and was found guilty of murder in the first degree without recommendation of mercy by the court.

He is returning today to the penitentiary at Salt Lake to await the trial of the murder of his wife. Bothe is in the custody of Chris, Christensen.

NOVEMBER 21, 1902

The Grand Valley Times

Bothe Sentenced

TO BE SHOT UNTIL DEAD
ON THE 29TH DAY OF NEXT MONTH

Shows Much Indifference

Charles Bothe was taken through here Tuesday from Monticello where he had been taken from the state penitentiary to receive sentence for his crime of last April or thereabouts.

Dutch Charley, the name he is generally known by, was found guilty of the murder of his wife and Wm. Tibbetts and received the sentence to be shot on the 29th of December of this year.

As he left here he seemed as cool and indifferent as if he was going to live for 50 years more. When leaving the jail he asked Chris. Christensen, the man who had him in charge, when the d_ _n thing was going to come off.

At all times, even when he went through here before, he seemed to be as unconscious of the horrible crime he committed as well as the punishment which he is about to receive.

This same man is said to have confessed to killing two men in Germany, the place of his berth, and two in Telluride, Colo.

CHAPTER 3

THE WIDOW'S SON

FTER THE MURDER OF HER HUSBAND, Amy Tibbetts and her two small sons were alone on the ranch near old La Sal. Amy had family in Moab, but Moab was forty miles away over dirt roads and wooden wagon wheels. Some of her friends and family suggested that she move to town, but Amy wouldn't do that. The little cabin in the wilderness was her home and she refused to leave it. She and Bill had dreamed of building a fine ranch there, with a beautiful home, and she wouldn't let the dream die. Somehow, she would build that ranch with her sons and it would be a tribute to the life of the man she had loved so dearly.

Few people carried life insurance in those days, but Amy still had the land and the cattle to secure her future. She knew that if she left the ranch, her cattle would be scattered and the processes of nature would soon destroy her hard-won gains. Ditches required cleaning and fences needed mended. Also, if she moved to town, it was possible that some devious person might file a counter-claim on her land, insisting that she had abandoned the homestead. She had heard of such things happening to others. Amy was sure she could beat such a claim in court, but it might be a long and costly process and she wasn't up to the fight. Better to stay and hold on to what she had.

But it was serious business to be a widow on the frontier, especially a widow with small children to care for. The demands of the cattle business required the full-time efforts of a good man. A woman with children just couldn't do it alone.

Amy was making plans to enlist her brothers as partners when another cruel twist of fate intervened. She found that she was in debt. Her late husband had been charging goods at the general store in old La Sal, promising to settle up when his steers were marketed in the fall. It was a common practice. The store was owned by the Cross-H Cattle Company where Bill had worked as a seasonal employee.

And then, like a thunderbolt of bad luck, a cowboy she didn't know came to her door with a note stating that her recently deceased husband owed him two hundred dollars. Two hundred dollars was a lot of money, most of a year's wages for common folks. The man said that if she didn't have the money he would be happy to take the land or the cattle to settle the debt. If not, he would see her in court.

Amy was convinced that the note was a forgery. Bill had never told her he was indebted to anyone. He was a man who prided himself on being self-reliant and she just couldn't imagine him borrowing that much money from a cowboy and not a bank. Yet, in spite of her doubts, everyone agreed that the signature on the note looked like her late husband's handwriting.

For months, Amy resisted desperately, but finally, disheartened, still mourning the loss of her husband, and with her spirit broken, she reluctantly signed the property over to the cowboy. She just didn't have the heart to fight the man in court. Amy loved her ranch, but the more practical choice was to give up the land and keep the cows. The cows could provide an income for her and her sons and maybe the start for a new ranch. There was still land available for homesteading in the San Juan area, but it took years to build up a good herd of cattle. Amy cried when she signed her property away, but she knew she was making the right choice. She had to take care of her little boys.

Her suspicions about being cheated were reinforced when the new owner of her property quickly sold it to the Cross-H Ranch. The Cross-H had offered to buy the land from her late husband several times, but he had always refused. The Tibbetts Ranch was in a prime location with a good spring of water and a natural meadow that was perfect for livestock. Amy believed until her dying day that she had been swindled.

The young widow moved with her children to Moab, but had to sell off a good portion of her remaining assets to pay her debts and get settled in town. The following items appeared in the Moab newspaper in 1904.

APRIL 23, 1904

The Grand Valley Times

ESTATE OF WILLIAM TIBBETTS, DECEASED

The undersigned will sell at private sale 66 head of range cattle, 8 saddle horses, with riding equipment, 1 30-30 rifle and scabbard, on or after May 13, 1904.

Written bids will be received at Monticello, Utah. Terms of sale cash.

Fred N. Prewer, Administrator, Fist Pub, April 23rd, last May 13th, 1904.

APRIL 15, 1904

The Grand Valley Times

Sheriff Woods and deputy, of San Juan county passed through Moab, Tuesday of their way to Salt Lake City. Their mission is to get Charles Bothe, "Dutch Charlie" and bring him back to Monticello to be re-sentenced for the Tibbetts murder.

APRIL 22, 1904

The Grand Valley Times

The District Court had less than an hour's work in San Juan County, this term. Charles Bothe, the murderer of Wm. Tibbetts, who the Supreme Court remanded to the District Court for re-sentencing, was brought down from Salt Lake City, across the country in a wagon for 100 miles to be simply told that on June 10th, 1904 the sheriff would execute him, at the penitentiary at Salt Lake City.

JUNE 10, 1904

The Grand Valley Times

Sheriff Woods, of San Juan County, reached Moab the first part of the week, he was on his way to Salt Lake City to carry out the sentence imposed on Charles Bothe. While here he received the intelligence that Bothe's sentence had been commuted to life in prison.

Shortly after moving to Moab, Amy became reacquainted with an old friend from her school days. Wilford Wesley Allred, known as "Winny" to his friends, was two years younger than Amy, but he had been one of her suitors before she married the cowboy, Bill Tibbetts. Winny was still single and he stopped by often to visit and help with chores around her place. It wasn't long before he and Amy were married.

Winny Allred was a good man, but much different from Amy's first husband. He was a town person who made his living as a musician. His family ran a few cows on the rangeland near Moab, but Winny was more at home wearing a silk necktie than a cowboy's bandana.

After Winny and Amy were married, the young man worked hard to provide for his family and make his new wife happy. He was devoted to her and always wanted her to have the best of everything.

For a while, the new couple lived in Moab, but Amy grew restless living in town. Her heart was on the desert. She had been happy in her wilderness cabin at old La Sal and she longed for the red rocks and open spaces. She was a woman of strong will, and in spite of her

Wilford Wesley Allred

new husband's objections, Amy took her remaining cows and filed for a homestead in Brown's Hole, on the west side of the La Sal Mountains, about twenty miles southeast of Moab. It was a good place to start a new ranch and a second chance to live her dream. With charm and firm resolve, she was able to win her new husband over and he helped her build a log cabin there. They planted a big garden and fruit trees. The family lived there for several years and ran their cattle in the foothills of the mountain.

The cabin at Brown's Hole was very small in the early years, and with new babies arriving, there wasn't enough room for everyone to have a bed. The older boys, the stepsons, Bill Jr. and his little brother Joe, had to sleep in a corncrib outside of the cabin at night. Big gaps in the walls of the shed-like structure allowed air to circulate and dry the corn.

Miles of wilderness surrounded the homestead, and the boys were terrified at night by the howls of coyotes and the shrieks of mountain lions not far from where they lay huddled. The big cats sounded like a woman screaming in the night. Navajos have called it the Moki scream, and they say it is made by the spirits of dead people who once lived in the cliff dwellings of the canyon country. To adults who have heard the sound, the experience is unnerving. To little boys, all alone in the dark, peeking out at the night through the gaps of a flimsy corn shed, the experience was a holy terror.

To please his new wife, Winny Allred went through the motions of being a cowboy and a farmer, but he wasn't happy. His heart was still in town. He and Amy were not a good match when it came to setting up housekeeping in the wilderness. In spite of the homestead, the cows, and the demands of taming the frontier, Winny still tried to make his living as a musician. The job required that he spend a lot of time in town. He worked hard to be a good provider, but he was torn between the obligations to his family and the demands of his chosen profession. It was a conflict that would trouble his marriage, his family, and his life, for many years.

There were other problems in the family, too. For six-year-old Bill Tibbetts Jr., the marriage of his mother to a strange man was a distressing experience. The little boy wouldn't accept it. He had fond memories of his father and he refused to acknowledge his mother's new husband as anything but an interloper who threatened the sovereignty of what was left of his family.

As time progressed, the conflict between little Bill and his stepfather steadily grew worse. Bill was an active, impatient, and strong-willed little boy and he simply refused to accept this new guy as dad. Winny Allred was a strict disciplinarian and he was constantly at odds with the boy. Bill was spanked a lot. The beatings only deepened the boy's hatred and resolve. Bill openly vowed that one day, when he was older, he would beat the hell out of his stepfather. The rivalry between the two became so intense that Amy finally sent little Bill to live with her parents in Moab. It was the only way to keep peace in the family.

And so, at the age of seven, Bill lost his mother to another man. He didn't have a place in his mother's new family. On top of witnessing the violent death of his father when he was only four, this new reality hit him like a hammer.

Bill remained committed to his mother, even though he didn't get to see her very often after moving to Moab. The separation only increased his hatred for the man who had come between them. The little boy pouted and sulked.

At Moab, Bill's grandparents, Joseph and Hanna Moore, became major influences in his young life. They owned a farm along the edge of town where they grew their own food and hand-made most of the items needed to sustain their lives. They were proud and independent people, and very religious. Joseph Moore had been a Mormon bishop in the town of Bennington, Idaho, in the 1870s.

Bill's grandparents took him to church every Sunday and taught him all about right and wrong, the importance of being honest, and the value of keeping his word. They took him to Sunday School and read to him from the Bible and The Book of Mormon in the evenings. Shortly after his eighth birthday, they made sure that he was properly baptized, by immersion, in the cold and muddy water of the Colorado River.

Young Bill got along much better with his grandfather than he did with his stepfather, and a couple of his uncles took the little boy under their wings and became adult role models, as well. Little Bill and his Uncle Ephraim Moore developed a special bond. It was Ephraim who had acted as midwife when Bill was born and the two became like brothers. It didn't matter that Ephraim was eighteen years older.

But it was an older uncle, Will Moore, who became Bill's father figure. Will was an old-time cowboy, strong, proud, and as tough as saddle leather. He reminded the little boy of his dad. Bill grew up idolizing his cowboy Uncle Will.

One of the advantages of living in town was going to school. Bill liked school and he became a good student, learning to read and write very well. He was interested in history, science, and literature. He read all of the books available to him at school and the home of his grandparents. Many of his grandparent's books were religious texts, so the boy was no stranger to the stories of the Bible.

To get to school, Bill had to walk past the Jackson place. The Jackson boys were older and bigger than Bill, and the two of them would lie in wait for the skinny new kid and beat him up, almost every day. The older boys thought it was great sport and they carried it to extremes.

Little Bill was terrorized by the bullying. He became afraid to go to school and afraid to go out to play. Finally, when the situation became obvious to the adults, Uncle Will took him aside for some intensive training in the manly arts of self-defense.

"It's not the size of the man in the fight that counts," the tough cowboy said. "It's the size of the fight in the man. Those guys are bigger than you, but you can beat them if you set your mind to it. You can't worry about being hurt. They're going to hurt you anyway. You might as well attack and give some back. If you hurt them, they'll learn to leave you alone. Here's what to do the next time they start that stuff…"

It worked like a charm. Within just a few days, Bill had conquered the Jackson boys. He then beat up the big kid down the lane and a bully on the playground. His newfound assertiveness won him a lot of friends and a lot of attention at school. His self-confidence soared and he learned to swagger just a little. By the time he was ten, he had a reputation for being the toughest kid in school. Bill might have even gone a little too far when he discovered how easy it was to intimidate people. Over the next few years he tried every new kid in school, just so everyone would know who was boss.

FROM LEFT: *Ephraim and Will Moore*

Bill's defiance of his stepfather, his constant fighting at school, and his need to be the top dog among his peers, might suggest that he had some deep emotional wounds to heal. The little boy had witnessed the murder of his father, the loss of his home, his mother's new marriage to a man he despised, and the pain of being sent away from the family to live in a strange town with relatives. He surely felt wronged, rejected, angry, and afraid. There were no grief counselors or therapists in places like Moab in those days and life was hard. Little boys were taught that men never cry, no matter what.

But all of that pent-up emotion, frustration, and anger had to go somewhere. If he couldn't cry, he had to strike out, somehow. Young Bill Tibbetts became the toughest, and maybe the meanest, kid in Moab.

CHAPTER 4

A CHILD OF THE WILDERNESS

CHILDHOOD DIDN'T LAST LONG ON THE Utah frontier. Kids as young as five and six had chores to do around the house and barn, and most began working in the fields before they were ten. Agriculture was a very labor-intensive occupation in the days of horse-drawn farm machinery and the whole family was involved in making a living.

While living with his grandparents on their farm in Moab, Bill learned all about hard work and responsibility at an early age. He milked the cows, cleaned the chicken coop, and chopped his share of the firewood. He learned the farming business by digging in the dirt, and his uncles taught him the skills of a cowboy. By his teenage years, he was an accomplished horseman who could throw a rope with the best of them.

While still a boy of tender age, Bill began working for the Murphy Cattle Company, a large ranching enterprise headquartered in Moab. With the Murphy outfit he spent his summers in the land between the Green and Colorado rivers, the Big Flat, Upheaval Dome, and Island in the Sky country north and west of Moab. Part of that cattle range is now the northern end of Canyonlands National Park. The land was raw, wild, and undeveloped when Bill first saw it, and he fell in love with the place.

It was not unusual in those days for boys as young as ten or twelve to work for the big cow outfits. Boys that young might have been too small to rope steers and wrestle calves for the branding iron, but they could ride a horse and help move livestock to greener pastures. Kids also worked as camp tenders, gathering firewood, fetching water, wrangling horses, and helping the chuckwagon cook. They helped to set up and take down the camp, peel potatoes, wash dishes, harness the team, and tend a few doggie calves. Sometimes there was even a cow to milk.

OPPOSITE: *The Portal view from Moab Valley*

Bill in his early 20s

Part of Bill's job with the Murphy cattle outfit was digging out waterholes and making small earthen dams to catch runoff water for the cows. To do this, he ran a Fresno, a large, metal-bladed wooden scoop that was pulled behind a horse or a team of horses. Fresnos were the principal tools of road and railroad construction in those days. Operating one would have been a big job for a kid. The machine was called a Fresno because they were manufactured in Fresno, California, and the word "Fresno" was painted on the sideboards.

In the early 1900s, when Bill worked for the cattle company, much of the land in southeast Utah was still untamed, unnamed, unmapped, and unexplored. Even the old-timers often had no clue about what was at the head of the canyon or around the next bend of the river. To a bold and adventurous boy like Bill Tibbetts, the place was magic. Buffalo Bill and his Wild West Show offered nothing young Bill couldn't find in his own backyard. In the canyons around Moab, real old-time cowboys still bucked-out wild horses and chased long-horned cattle with bullwhips and ropes. Renegade bands of non-reservation Utes and Paiutes still skulked in the mountain shadows, while up any side canyon might be a major cliff dwelling, a lost city of stone ten thousand years old.

Somewhere in the canyons there was sure to be a vein of pure silver or gold, eight or ten feet thick, or a lost Spanish mine, or Montezuma's hidden treasure. There were caves to explore, ancient Indian picture writings to decipher, and deer and mountain sheep waiting to be hunted for camp meat. There were arrowheads scattered around the waterholes and colorful nodules of agate and quartzite littering the hillsides. Whole petrified trees were lying just as they fell when the Biblical flood of Noah knocked them to the ground. There were catfish in the river, herds of antelope on the grasslands, rattlesnakes in the rocks, and eagles nesting on the mesa tops. The world was new and the whole country waited impatiently to be explored.

Young Bill did his best to see it all. On horseback and on foot he traversed the canyons and the mesas, exploring ruins, climbing to the top of rocky overlooks, peeking into dark caves and fissures in the rocks, following watercourses and game trails over the canyon rims. He traveled the cowboy and outlaw trails, discovering where they began and where they ended. He learned to navigate the canyon country and keep track of where he was by keeping a bearing on the sun and prominent landmarks on the horizon. His guideposts were the snowy tips of the La Sal Mountains to the east, the Blue Mountains to the south, the hazy peaks of the Henry Mountains far to the southwest, and the long ridge of the Book Cliffs to the north. At night, while camping out for weeks on end, he memorized the night sky, watching the constellations circle the North Star as the moon pirouetted through her phases.

As a boy, Bill learned to survive in the desert. His uncles taught him to follow game trails to find hidden sources of water deep in the canyons, and he learned to dig in the damp sand against the ledges to tease a drink of water from a tiny seep of a spring. He learned which desert plants were edible and which ones would kill a horse. He learned to dig sego bulbs and Indian potatoes, how to gather pinyon nuts and eat a prickly pear cactus. He learned how to catch a rabbit by using a forked stick or a length of barbed wire to pull it from its den. He learned to trap, hunt, and prepare wild game for the cooking pot. He learned how to camp and sleep comfortably at night without a bedroll or blankets. He discovered that he could go all day without a drink of water, and two or three days without food, if he had to. Growing up on the desert made him tough and self-reliant.

By his mid-teenage years, Bill was a survivalist. He could live on the desert like an ancient Paiute, relying solely on wit, instinct, and woodcraft. His survival skills and intimate knowledge of the canyon country would serve him well in the years to come.

<hr />

Sometime in those early years, Bill discovered a hidden cave in an area known today as Arches National Park. He used a rope and an oiled-rag torch to explore the cave by himself, and he carved his name on an interior wall. In 1946, he took his sons there to show them his secret place. His youngest son, Ray, carved his name in the cave beneath his father's 1917 inscription. The cave remained a Tibbetts family secret until it was found by hikers and reported to the park service in 1987, some seventy years after Bill had carved his name there.

LEFT TO RIGHT: *Tse-ne-gat (Poke's son); Jess Posey (Posey's son); Anson Posey (Posey's son); Posey; Poke.*

CHAPTER 5

INDIAN WARS, HORSE THIEVES, AND OUTLAWS

IN THE SPRING OF 1915, BILL TIBBETTS TURNED seventeen. His school days were behind him and he was almost a man. He was growing up and growing restless in the small town of Moab and yearning to seek his fortune in the wide world of high adventure. Like most teenage boys in the first blush of young adulthood, he was feeling cocky, rebellious, and bulletproof. His troubled mood fit the troubled times.

Around the world, 1915 was a year of war and trouble. In Europe, the First World War was in its second year. Millions of men from many nations were fighting and dying in the muddy trenches of France and Belgium. American newspapers were full of shrill alarms and biased yellow journalism. Headlines spotlighted the evils of Kaiser Wilhelm and his spike-helmeted German troops. Editors and army generals were rattling sabers, but the country wouldn't enter the war for another two years. South of the border, Mexico was deep in revolution. Pancho Villa and his men were seizing control of the country. Closer to Moab, there was an Indian uprising in progress.

The Indian "war" of 1915 began when a San Juan County Ute, named Tse-ne-gat (meaning Crybaby, or One Who Cries a Lot), was charged with the murder of a Mexican sheepherder in Colorado. When Tse-ne-gat refused to voluntarily surrender to authorities in Utah, a rowdy and allegedly drunken civilian posse was sent to track him down. The posse was assembled in Colorado under the command of a U.S. Marshal.

The Colorado posse surrounded an Indian camp near the town of Bluff, Utah, in the early morning hours of February 20, 1915, and quickly got into a shootout with Tse-ne-gat and some of his Ute and Paiute relatives. A posse member was killed and two others wounded. One of the Indians was armed with a very modern 30-06 rifle and it took a while for the white guys to learn to fully appreciate the range and capabilities of the weapon. But the posse did a little better against the non-combatants in the Indian camp. According to newspapers, "a squaw and two papooses" were killed in the ambush and two "old warriors" were captured. Tse-ne-gat and a small group of armed and dangerous Indians escaped to the south toward Navajo Mountain. The Indian camp was burned.

Another group of five Indian men from a nearby "peaceful" Indian camp voluntarily surrendered to avoid the conflict, but one of them was shot and killed by a civilian guard while "trying to escape." At the time, people in the town of Bluff called it a cold-blooded murder. The murdered Indian, a Ute named Havane, was well known and well respected in the little community. The trigger-happy guard was never charged with the murder. In fact, no one could explain why the "peaceful" Indians were being held under armed guard without being charged with a crime.

Shooting Indians was exciting stuff. There hadn't been a good Indian war in southeast Utah since the 1880s and the whites were due to win one. They had lost the last two: the "Pinhook Massacre" of 1881, and the Fight at Soldier Crossing in 1884. Newspaper reporters caught the spirit of the thing, and, from the headlines of the day, the whole country was made to believe that San Juan County was in a full-fledged Indian war. The towns of Blanding and Bluff were said to be under siege, and dozens, maybe hundreds, of "hostile redskins" were lurking on the edge of town, lusting for white scalps. The whole country was up in arms and newspapers everywhere were screaming for federal troops.

In response to the threat, The War Department sent an army general to quell the Indian uprising. To everyone's surprise, the wise and experienced old soldier came without cannons or soldiers. In just a matter of days, General Hugh L. Scott, through the aid of native interpreters, was able to sweet-talk old Tse-ne-gat and his father, Old Poke, along with another Paiute chieftain, Old Posey, into surrendering.

Tse-ne-gat agreed to be sent to Colorado to face the murder charges. But before he was sent to Denver for trial, Tse-ne-gat and the other "renegades" were compelled to meet with the governor of Utah and his entourage in the town of Bluff for a big "Pow-wow" and photo opportunity. Someone had to take credit for winning the "Indian war."

Tse-ne-gat faced an all-white jury in the federal court in Denver. The evidence was weak and he was quickly acquitted. He returned home a free man. But while he was still being held in federal custody, Tse-ne-gat and three other "Indian troublemakers" were taken to Salt Lake City on a train to be paraded as trophies of the white man's victory. The natives were given a grand tour of the city with newsmen, politicians, and photographers following them everywhere. Then, after promising the governor that they would be good Indians from then on, the "defeated red men" were taken back to southern Utah and released into the wild.

———•◦•———

That's how things were in the spring of 1915. There was lots of talk about war, murder, rampaging Indians, hate and revenge. It was an exciting time for a couple of teenaged boys to be camping out on the cattle ranges, all alone and far from the nearest settlement. In their youthful imaginations, there might be a "war-painted savage" behind any rock or bush. Young Bill Tibbetts and his friend Carlisle Dalton kept a sharp eye out.

The young cowboys had been in the Big Flat country, near Island in the Sky, for three or four weeks. It was calving time and they were working for the Murphy Cattle Company. The boys were about the same age and they had become good friends over the past several months. They were sitting around an evening campfire when Bill spoke.

"What ya gonna do on payday, Carlisle? We've each got about twenty dollars comin'."

Carlisle Dalton thought about it for a moment, poking at the campfire with a stick. Dancing flames cast moving shadows over his suntanned young face and his mood was quiet and somber. "I've been thinkin' about goin' home," he said. "I haven't seen my family in Parowan for a long time. I think I'd like to go home."

"I've never been to Parowan," Bill mused. "I haven't been hardly anywhere except to La Sal and Monticello. Of course, I did see Green River when we took steers up there to put on the train. Those big ol' steam engines are somethin', I'm tellin' you."

"Well, Parowan is a lot different than Moab," Carlisle said as he tossed another stick on the fire. "Parowan is in a big old valley with lots of grass and none of these darn bottomless canyons to cross. They ain't got all this sand to wade in, either. And I don't remember the gnats being as fierce and starved as these critters. They got civilized bugs over in Parowan. Yes sir, and that's a fact."

"I've never seen any civilized bugs," Bill smiled.

"And they've got some real purdy girls over in Parowan, too," Carlisle said with an impish grin, "Real healthy girls." "Holsteins," he said, holding his cupped hands in front of his chest. "Not like those skinny things around Moab. I ought to take you over there and introduce you to some of my cousins. You'd throw rocks at Sally Tucker if I introduced you to my cousin Elsie."

"Oh, knock it off," Bill growled, trying hard not to smile. "I only danced with her twice before her momma took her home bawlin' like a lost calf."

"Yea, she's sweet on you, all right. Too bad she's only thirteen. I think if you ever ask her to dance again, her momma is gonna run over you like a wild-eyed old range cow, all stompin' and blowin' snot. You better be careful around that Tucker girl, my friend."

"Aw, what can I say?" Bill grinned. "I'm such a handsome buck. The women just can't resist me. It runs in the family, you know. My momma says my old man was about the handsomest bull calf this side of the Paradox Valley, and I got his steely gray eyes. The girls just can't leave me alone."

"Ain't you somethin'," Carlisle spat as he scooped up a handful of sand and threw it across the fire at Tibbetts. "Go get some firewood, you handsome bastard. I'll stay here by the fire and try to keep the girls out of camp."

Bill ducked and laughed out loud. "Maybe you better introduce me to your cousin Elsie," he teased. "If I married her, we'd be in-laws as well as outlaws and you could invite us over for supper every Sunday afternoon. I'll go all the way to Parowan with you if you'll show me cousin Elsie and those civilized bugs you've been braggin' about."

"You got a deal," Carlisle said. "After we settle up with old man Murphy, we're on the road to Parowan. I just hope cousin Elsie doesn't see you comin' and go stampedin' off down the valley. A homely feller like you might have to sneak up on a purdy girl like Elsie. Elsie is a perfect model of high-class culture and refinement and those snoopy gray eyes of yours will get your face slapped in a hurry, you mark my word. And her momma is a real wildcat compared to that lame and tame old momma cow who claims Sally Tucker. You try to kiss cousin Elsie and her momma will nut you with a dull deer horn, and that's a fact."

Hoots of laughter echoed out over the sand flats in the darkness. The hobbled horses raised their heads and looked back toward the firelight and the source of the happy sounds. Far off in the bottom of the canyon a coyote yipped and then howled mournfully. The innocent and care-free days of youth were almost at an end for the two young cowboys. Tomorrow would be a new day and the beginning of sorrows.

⎯⎯⎯·•·⎯⎯⎯

A few days later, the boys left Moab early in the morning. It was dark and the streets were empty. They had ropes and canvas slickers tied to their saddles and Bill had appropriated an extra horse from his stepfather's corral to carry a light camp outfit. He didn't ask permission to take the animal.

Winny Allred would surely be annoyed by his stepson's insolence, but the teenager had done such things before, knowing that his stepfather would do nothing about it. Allred thought more of keeping the peace with his strong-willed wife than bickering with her smart-alecky oldest son. Bill took full advantage of the situation and thoroughly enjoyed tormenting his stepfather.

The young men crossed the river on the new iron bridge without meeting any other travel-ers. A dog barked from near a squatter's shack as they crossed Courthouse Wash and followed the road along the river. The sun finally spilled over the mountains and splashed down on them as they turned the horses up Moab Canyon, headed north.

"How much money you got, Bill?" Carlisle asked.

"Little over seven dollars."

"That ain't much to be showin' off for cousin Elsie with," Carlisle teased.

"I had to finish payin' off this saddle," Bill replied. "And I had to buy me a new shirt. Gotta look good fer cousin Elsie, you know. I gave my grandma a couple a bucks to help with the gro-ceries, too. She's been real good to me. She didn't want me to go on this trip with you, either," Bill said with a big grin. "She said I'd just be getting into trouble goin' all the way to Parowan with an outlaw like you."

Carlisle smiled but didn't say anything.

"I think we ought to take a shortcut," Bill said as they neared the top of Moab Canyon. "Uncle Will says it's a long ways to Parowan if we follow the road through Green River, Price, and Salina. I think we ought to follow the old Horsethief Trail down to the Green River at the

Moab Bridge across the Colorado River

mouth of Mineral Canyon. We can cross the river there, and Hanksville is just across the Robbers Roost, somewhere over near Factory Butte. I ain't ever been there before, but Uncle Eph pointed out the landmarks last year when we took some of his steers to Green River to sell. I'm sure I can find the place. From Hanksville, they say there's a good road that goes west along the Fremont River toward the settlements in Iron County. I think it might be shorter to go that way and we can go swimmin' in the river, too."

"I've never been down the Horsethief Trail or through the Robbers Roost," Carlisle confessed. "But if you say it's the best way, then I'm all for it. By the way, why do they call it the Horsethief Trial?"

"Uncle Ephraim says the trail was used by a bunch of horse thieves back in the early days," Bill explained. "The outlaws were usin' the trail to steal horses from the ranchers near Moab. The bad guys would sneak up on the mesa, steal the horses, and then go back down the trail to hide out in the Robbers Roost."

"Are those outlaws still out there on the Roost somewhere?" Carlisle asked.

"No," Bill said. "Eph claims the ranchers caught some of them and hanged them in the cottonwoods down along the river near Tidwell Bottom. They never contacted the sheriff or anything; just hanged the outlaws and buried them in the sand along the river. Most people never knew anything about it. Eph said it was easier that way. The ranchers didn't have to go to a lot of bother with a trial and all. After that, the outlaws went someplace else to steal horses."

At the top of Moab Canyon, not far from a stagecoach stop called Courthouse Station, the boys left the well-traveled road and turned west up Seven Mile Canyon. They were going to the high mesa country where they'd been tending cows just a few days before. They camped that afternoon near a water hole in the Big Flat country on top of the mesa.

Early the next morning, the eastern sky was awash in brilliant orange when a band of horses came to the stock pond for a cold drink of water. The boys were squatting around a smoky campfire, frying bacon and dough-gob biscuits in a small iron skillet and trying to get warm. They recognized the horses. They had seen them many times before. The animals ran free in the high mesa country even though they were domestic stock and not wild mustangs. Ranchers often turned "extra" horses loose to forage for themselves. Running free on the range for a year or two was a great way to teach a colt to be sure-footed in the rough country.

"Those are sure some pretty horses, ain't they, Carlisle?"

"Yeah," the Dalton boy agreed. "I think that big sorrel is one of old Doc William's horses. He had him in town for a while, if that's the same horse, and I think it is."

"Wouldn't it be somethin' to have so many horses you could just turn half-a-dozen of 'em loose to run with the cows out here?" Bill sighed. "It sure doesn't seem fair. I had to work almost two years to buy this one little mare of mine, her and the saddle, of course."

"I wonder how many of those range horses those rich guys lose to lions and wolves and such," Carlisle questioned.

"And outlaws," Bill reminded him. "There's been many a good horse stolen out here on the open range."

There was a long and heavy silence as the boys watched the horses drinking at the pond. Then young Bill spoke quietly, and very matter of fact. "We could steal that bunch of horses purdy darn easy, ya know. The sheriff and all of those rich guys are down in San Juan County chasin' those Indians around, tryin' to get their pictures in the newspapers."

"That's a fact," Carlisle agreed. "And with all of the Indian troubles in the district this spring, I'm sure that old Posey, or that other buck, old Senna-guts, or whatever his name is, would be happy to take the blame. Them Injuns is horse stealin' fools."

"By darn, we could do it, couldn't we?" Bill said quietly, thinking it over.

"I'll bet they're worth four hundred dollars," Carlisle said, beginning to sound excited. "Even that colt would bring a good price. You could sure show cousin Elsie a good time with that much money, and that's a fact."

"What would we do with 'em?"

"We could sell them in the settlements over in Iron County," Carlisle said eagerly. "Nobody from Moab ever goes over there. Besides, it might take old Doc Williams and those other rich guys months to miss those range horses. And when they do, they'll just figure the Indians got 'em or the wolves ate 'em up and scattered the bones."

"I wonder where old man Murphy's cowboys are workin' this week," Bill said in a sneaky tone of voice. "Let's ride to the top of the ridge and see if there's anybody around."

The sun hadn't peaked in the noonday sky before the boys dropped off the steep rim of the canyon, headed down the Horsethief Trail. Before them they drove eight fine-looking horses, all sweaty and covered with foam. Bill was still leading the packhorse he had commandeered from his step-father. In the eyes of the law, that made nine.

From a high rim above the river, the boys paused to look down on that wide expanse of desert and canyons known as the Robbers Roost. It was the last wild remnant of the Old West, the former hideout and wilderness sanctuary of such notables as Butch Cassidy, Harry Longabaugh, Tom Dilly, and Matt Warner. By late afternoon, the young horse thieves had crossed the river, headed west. Later that night their campfire was the only light to be seen anywhere in the six hundred square miles of the Robbers Roost.

———

Early the next morning, the boys started west to find the Hanksville road. Not knowing the country, they followed a trail Bill was familiar with, the cow trail that took Ephraim's cows to market in the town of Green River. Bill had been over the route the previous fall and he remembered the landmarks. The cow trail took them farther north than they wanted to be, but it would put them on the Hanksville road near the San Rafael River.

Late that afternoon, as they approached the San Rafael, they heard shooting coming from the direction of the river. The boys rode to the top of a ridge to check it out. Below them they saw an old man running across a plowed field while two men with rifles were shooting

SEPTEMBER 10, 1915

The Grand Valley Times

Two Boy's Rash Act

18-YEAR-OLD LADS LEAVE COUNTY WITH 9 OTHER PEOPLES' HORSES.

Carlisle Dalton of Parowan, who has spent the past two years at Moab, and William Tibbets, son of the late William Tibbets of La Sal, both about eighteen years of age, have made an auspicious beginning to what may develop into two careers in crime, unless they are apprehended and shown the error of their ways. Sometime during June, these young men left Moab, intending it is understood, to ride to Iron County. On their way they gathered up nine head of horses that were running on the Big Flat west of Moab, and took them with them. Four of the horses belong to R. Lee Kirk, four to Dr. J. W. Williams, and one to W. W. Allred. The two boys sold seven of the animals at Hanksville and two at Parowan.

The theft of the horses was not discovered until about two months later, when some of the animals were seen in the Hanksville section and it was then learned that the two young men had sold them there.

A warrant for the young men's arrest was issued from the sheriff's office. The Dalton boy was apprehended at Parowan and Deputy R.C. Clark left for that place the first of the week to bring him to Moab. The Tibbets boy has not been found, although the sheriffs office is conducting a diligent search for him.

THE EASTERN UTAH ADVOCATE

SHOOT DESPERADO IN SELF-DEFENSE

Bill Hatfield of Famous Allen Gang of Kentucky Slain by Utahns

Was Drinking and Started Out Looking for Trouble, Beginning the Shooting When Ordered Off the Place By Ranchers

Salt Lake City – Special to the Tribune from Green River, Utah says William Hatfield of the Hatfield and Allen Gang of Kentucky, alias Bill Chisholm better known through eastern Utah as "Shoot-em-up Bill," one of the most daring and desperate gunmen of eastern Utah, was shot and killed twelve miles south of Green River in a duel with William Tomlinson and James Warner, two ranch boys on the San Rafael river. A Coroner's jury has acquitted Hatfield's slayers.

Hatfield left Green River Monday with several gallons of whiskey for the San Rafael Reef, where he had camped on some mining property that he was working. On reaching camp he began drinking heavily and Wednesday decided to clean up and have a few funerals of his own. Hanging a Winchester rifle on his saddle and loading a 38 colts revolver he started out on horseback to do things up on the opposite side of the river.

Stopping at a farm house just across the bridge he informed a young woman that he intended to shoot up a few fellows on that side of the stream that day. By this time Louis and Felix Pressett came around the house to see what the trouble was.

They ordered Hatfield off the place and during the quarrel which ensued Hatfield pointed his gun at them and stated he was going to clean up the place. Two neighbor boys hearing the quarrel, came to the Pressetts' assistance. Each carried a Winchester and ordered Hatfield off the farm. A shower of bullets was Hatfield's answer. During the exchange of shots the wild Kentuckian fell from his horse dead. Two bullets had passed through his body.

at him from the edge of the field. As they watched, the old man staggered, stumbled, and went down. To the young cowboys, it looked like a cold-blooded murder.

Not wanting to get mixed up in a murder, the boys went back to their stolen horses and very quickly got the hell out of there. They cut the Hanksville road in short order and went south as fast as they could travel.

Bill and Carlisle found out later they had witnessed one of the most famous shootings ever to happen in eastern Utah. The victim was a bad man known locally as Shoot-em-up Bill. His real name was William Hatfield, and he was said to be a member of the famous Hatfield clan from Kentucky who feuded with the McCoys. The story might have been true because the man was no stranger to gunplay. His bad hip and crooked jaw were reminders of old gunfights when he finished in second place. People said ol' Shoot-em-up always wore his six-guns, and he was always waving them around and threatening to kill people. There were rumors of a warrant for his arrest over in Colorado where he had killed a woman by mistake while fighting with her husband or boyfriend.

Shoot-em-up had come to Utah to seek his fortune prospecting in the Henry Mountains, but at the time of his death he was living in a dugout across the San Rafael River from the Tomlinson Ranch. It came out in a coroner's inquest that Shoot-em-up had gotten drunk that day and had gone to a neighboring farm where he was terrorizing an older couple with his guns, threats, and vile language. When another neighbor intervened, ol' Shoot-em-up took a shot at him, and missed.

It wasn't the first time farmers along the river had been tormented and bullied by the pistol packin' old scoundrel and they were tired of it. A couple of young men loaded their rifles, ran old Shoot-em-up down, and put him out of his misery.

An inquest was held in the town of Green River a few days later. A coroner's jury ruled that Shoot-em-up had met his death as the result of a justifiable homicide. The men who did the shooting were defending their homes and families and no charges were filed.

Ephraim Moore attended the inquest in Green River and heard the testimony of the shooting firsthand. But by the time the inquest was held, two unknown eyewitnesses, Bill Tibbetts and Carlisle Dalton, had passed through Hanksville and were basking in the promised land of Parowan with their pockets full of silver dollars.

SEPTEMBER 24, 1915

The Grand Valley Times

WILL BE TRIED IN MANTI

William Tibbets, the 17-year old Moab boy who with Carlisle Dalton is alleged to have stolen a number horses belonging to Dr. J. W. Williams, R. Lee Kirk and others, sometime in June, will be tried for the offense before Juvenile Judge E. D. Sorenson at Manti, Saturday, according to a telegram received by Sheriff Bliss from Deputy Sheriff R. C. Clark today.

Tibbets was captured by the sheriff of Iron county who telegraphed Sheriff Bliss, Tuesday, that he would take the boy to Salt Lake City and deliver him to the officers there. Deputy Sheriff Clark went to Salt Lake City to meet the Iron county officer and on his arrival there was directed by the Juvenile Judge to take the boy to Manti for trial.

OCTOBER 1, 1915

The Grand Valley Times

YOUNG MAN PLEADS GUILTY

William Tibbets on Friday plead guilty to complicity in the theft of a number of horses from Grand county people last June, before juvenile judge E.D. Sorenson at Manti. He was remanded to the state industrial school at Ogden.

Deputy Sheriff R.C. Clark who accompanied the young man from Salt Lake to Manti, returned to Moab Wednesday. He declares that young Tibbets asked Judge Sorenson to sell his Horse and saddle and turn the money over to the men from whom he took the horses last summer. The young man stated that as soon as he can, he intends to repay the men for the money they expended in getting their stock back.

APRIL 19, 1918

The Grand Valley Times

GRAND COUNTY ROLL OF HONOR

Earl Somerville, son of Mr. and Mrs. Andrew Somerville, and William Tibbets, son of Mrs. Wilford W. Allred, are both members of the regular army, having enlisted last winter in the coast artillery and being stationed at Fort Moultre, S.C. In letters home the boys state that they are enjoying life and are fast getting into good shape.

Mrs. Allred has another son in the service, Joseph (Dody) Tibbets, who is in the infantry and left a short time ago for France.

CHAPTER 6

A FAREWELL TO ARMS

IN EARLY SUMMER OF 1919, YOUNG BILL Tibbetts finally came home. After spending eighteen months at the Utah Sate Industrial School for juvenile offenders in Ogden, Utah, Bill had joined the army. He was nineteen when he put on the uniform. At the time, America was mobilizing to fight the First World War and Uncle Sam was happy to have a few healthy young juvenile delinquents join the ranks. The state of Utah thought it was a good idea, too. What better way to rehabilitate a kid than send him to the army?

Spending time in the army and traveling across the country gave Bill a whole new perspective of the world he lived in. In many ways, he was different when he came home to Moab. He was older, smarter, more world-wise, and more apt to think things through than he had been. He was twenty-one-years-old now, five feet, ten inches tall, and well muscled. His bearing, good looks, and commanding personality made him stand out in a crowd. Men stepped aside and women swooned.

But in some ways, the child of the desert hadn't changed much. He still liked to have a little fun and he was never one to turn down a dare. And he still loved to fight. Bill had been the champion boxer in his army unit. He would take on anybody, inside the ring or out. The toughest kid in Moab had been the toughest soldier at Fort Moultrie, South Carolina.

But now he was home. With juvenile detention and the army behind him, it was time to make a life for himself. Still wearing his army uniform, he went to visit his mother at the homestead in Brown's Hole.

They were sitting in wicker chairs under the cottonwoods, just the two of them, politely sipping glasses of lemonade, when Amy asked the big question.

"What are you going to do now, Bill?"

"I don't know, Mom. I've saved a little money, but I'm not sure what to do with it yet. I'd like to get a start in the cow business, the way you and Dad did before … well, you know. I think I'd like to run some cows. Trouble is, all the good range is taken. I don't know where to go to make a start."

"It's getting real tough around here." His mother said wistfully. "We've had cows on the foothills of South Mountain for almost fifteen years now and there seems to be more cows and more cowboys up there all the time. The range is really getting crowded. We've been losing a lot of calves, too. Rustling is getting out of hand in these parts. That's why your dad stayed on the range with the cows so much. We got neighbors who'll smile and offer their hand when they meet you face-to-face, but they'll steal your calves the minute you turn your back. Black-hearted, cussed damn people," she said, and then she smiled weakly with embarrassment and dropped her eyes as if she were ashamed for using such rough and irreverent language in front of her son. A blush came to her cheeks and she hid her face behind her glass of lemonade. "Your dad would have put a stop to it," she said from behind the glass.

"How many cows you got now?" he asked.

"Couple of hundred," she said proudly. "I'd have a lot more if I had any help taking care of them. Hired hands just don't do as good a job as I'd like, and with this batch of kids, I can't spend the time it takes to do it right."

She took another sip of lemonade and then quietly offered a suggestion. "Maybe we could partner up?" she said, hopefully. "You take care of my cows and I'll pay you in calves. It would surely help me and it would be a good way for you to get a start."

Bill promised he would look into it.

Eastern Utah was open range and it was all public domain. Anyone could get in the livestock business and run cows or sheep almost anywhere they wanted. There were few fences and few laws governing the use or misuse of the land. The law of the jungle prevailed. A rancher simply claimed a territory, put his stock there to graze, and then defended his "right" to use that ground against all comers. Those who were tough, determined, and willing to fight usually prevailed. Those who were timid, polite, and less aggressive usually didn't.

It was a dog-eat-dog world. Dozens of mini-range wars were going on at any given time on any given range. Cattlemen came and cattlemen went. The Taylor Grazing Act, a congressional mandate that created the Bureau of Land Management and put restrictions on where and how many cows an outfit could run, was still several years in the future. The act wouldn't become law until 1934. Until then, it was a free-for-all on the open range. Young Bill Tibbetts knew he was climbing into the lion's den when he decided to be a stockman.

Back in Moab, Bill had a long visit with his uncle, Ephraim Moore. Ephraim, too, was in the cow business. He was running a few hundred head on the White Rim below Island in the Sky and along the Green River bottoms, some thirty miles to the south and west of Moab.

"If you want to get in the cow business you can partner up with me," Ephraim offered as they sat on the porch, watching the afternoon sun melt into the fire of a desert sunset. "You help take care of my stock and I'll help you get started. We can each keep our own brands and just run our cows together. You own your cows and I own my cows. The two of us runnin' the herd would be a big help. We could watch out for each other and it'll save me the cost of payin' a hired man."

It was a good offer. Ephraim Moore was a good man to partner with. He knew the cow business and the desert around Moab. He knew the other stockmen in the area and the tone and the tenor of local politics and personalities, too. He knew the boundaries claimed by the various cow outfits and he was on good terms with his neighbors, a man with lots of friends and few enemies. Ephraim was known as an honest man, a devout Mormon Elder who went to church often and officiated at most of the baptisms and other church ordinances on behalf of the extended Moore family clan. Like most committed Mormons, he didn't drink, smoke, or gamble.

But there was a tough side to Ephraim Moore, as well. He played by the rules but never ducked a fight. People respected him. In 1898, while still just a kid, he had joined the U.S. Marine Corps during the Spanish-American War. He was a smaller man than Bill Tibbetts, but lean, wiry, and tough as nails. He didn't talk much, but when he did, people listened.

Surprisingly, in spite of frequent church attendance, having been raised on the frontier had given Eph a muleskinner's vocabulary. He sometimes used colorful cowboy cuss words, but never in the presence of polite company. He was the master of his emotions and he could control his tongue when he needed to, or wanted to. But then, sometimes the man just needed to cuss. It got the poison out of his system.

And while he was not a bad-looking fellow, Ephraim was never a lady's man. Like many of the old-time cowboys, he was a committed bachelor to the end of his days. Bachelorhood was a rare thing for a Mormon Elder in the early 1900s. Brigham Young had taught that it was a man's duty to marry and have as many children as possible to help build up the kingdom of God on earth.

But to his credit, while remaining single in spite of the matrimonial pressures exerted by his church, Ephraim was a man of impeccable virtue. He didn't frequent bordellos or the habitations of loose and painted women. He did have a few lady friends during the course of his life, but those he called friends were church-going spinsters, respectable widows, or grandmas of the highest order. No woman was ever able to rope, tie, and tame him. His cows and the desert were his life.

Ephraim Moore was forty years old in the summer of 1919, when he and Bill became partners. He was still young enough to spend weeks in the saddle, but getting too old to enjoy sleeping on the ground.

"I appreciate the offer to partner up with you," Bill said with real sincerity. "And I'll work hard, Eph. But I've promised Mother that I'd take her cows, too. They're stealin' her blind over on the La

Uncle Eph on the White Rim

Sals. That man of hers won't stay with the darn cows. He spends all of his time in town. Nero fiddlin' while Rome burns, you know. He never was a cowman, anyway. I've gotta get mother's stock outta there and take care of them while there's still some to save."

"I'm fine with that," Ephraim consented. After all, Bill's mother was his sister and it was all in the family. "The question is where to go to expand the operation. If you buy a few dozen cows to get started, and with your mother's stock, we'll have over 600 head. There ain't room for that many on the river bottoms where I've been runnin' and the White Rim is full up, too. And if we push any farther north we'll have to fight every cow outfit this side of the Book Cliffs.

"There's got to be someplace we can run a few hundred head," Bill insisted.

"I don't know," Eph mused. "All the range around here is all taken up. Everything on the Blue Mountain, Dry Valley, the Big Indian country, and everything north is filled up with cow outfits. And I don't think you could squeeze another cow into the La Sals. Some of those poor old critters are eatin' moss above timberline now. There just ain't no other place for them to go."

"What's it like over on the Robbers Roost? I remember the time me and you rode over there to get that stud horse from old man Biddlecome. That's big country over there. Is the Roost all taken up?"

"There ain't a lot of water on the Roost," Eph explained. "And what little there is, old Biddlecome's got all sewed up. I wouldn't want to crowd a guy like Biddlecome, anyway. Some guys are best not to mess with."

"What's south of Biddlecome?" Bill persisted. "From what I remember, it looked like cedar country way down along the river there. Is there any grass down that way?"

"I don't really know much about it," Eph confessed. "From what I've seen, it looks like more of the White Rim country - not a great place for cows, but doable, maybe. I've heard it called the 'Laterite' country. Don't know if anyone has cows down there or not. People from Hanksville, maybe. One thing for sure though, it'll be a rough somnabitch. That's rugged country down along the river there."

"Well, I guess we better go check it out," Bill said, very matter of fact. "If we're gonna get rich in the cattle business, we gotta find a spot to spread out. Can you go day after tomorrow? I got business in town tomorrow."

"Sure," Eph said. "I'll get the camp outfit together and check the shoes on the horses."

———— •♦• ————

Early the next afternoon, Bill walked into the pool hall on Moab's main street. He was still wearing his army uniform and his flat-brimmed campaign hat. He found the man he was looking for sitting backwards on a wooden chair, watching a pool game in progress. The man saw him come in and stood up to greet him with an extended hand and a weak but friendly smile. "Hello, Bill, I heard you was home. It's good to see you back." Everyone in the pool hall turned to see the handsome young soldier.

Bill ignored the offer of a handshake. "I wanna talk to you outside," he said with a loud voice and a cold, deliberate sneer, his hands planted firmly on his hips. The older man stood there in shock and bewilderment with his right hand still extended.

All activity slammed to a stop inside the pool hall. In the sudden silence the sounds of little kids playing in the street echoed through the pool hall. From somewhere across the room a man cleared his throat and put a heavy beer mug down on a tabletop. The clock on the wall thumped like a heartbeat in the silence of the room.

"Sure, Bill, let's go outside," his stepfather said very quietly, his brow wrinkled in deep apprehension, his eyes showing fear. Bill turned and walked back outside, the heels of his army boots clicking loudly on the rough board floor. The pool hall emptied into the street. People on the sidewalks hurried over to see what was going on. A crowd quickly gathered.

Outside in the dusty street, Bill took off his army coat and draped it over the porch railing. He carefully set his hat on top of the coat and removed his necktie. He then turned to his stepfather with his jaw set. "You used to beat hell outa me when I was just a little kid," he said with a dramatic air as he rolled up his sleeves. "And I swore that when I got big enough, I was gonna knock the shit out of you, Winny, old boy. Today is the day. You can take it like a man or I can chase you all over town, but after all these years, I'm here to take you down."

Winny Allred just stood there for a moment, alone as it were, there in the street, surrounded by a group of his life-long friends and acquaintances. He looked at Bill and then at his friends. None of his friends would look back at him. They all turned their heads or looked at the ground. His rough and ready stepson stood there grinning like an alligator, his fists clenched and his chin in the air, posturing like a confident young gladiator. The young soldier was twenty years younger than his stepfather, bigger, taller, stronger, and infinitely more experienced in the manly art of bare-knuckled boxing. The next move was up to Winny Allred. He didn't hesitate long.

"I'm not running from you, Bill," the older man said with real conviction. "You go ahead and beat me to death if it makes you feel any better, but I ain't runnin'."

Bill was instantly impressed, and so were the people standing around. Somehow, no one had expected to see such courage in the eyes and the stance of the town's best fiddle player.

{ 41 }

"But before we fight, there's some things I want to say," Winny said with a quivering chin below eyes that were fixed and steady. "There's two sides to every story, Bill. And you wasn't the sweetest little kitten in the litter. I took your mother in when she was widowed. She was alone with two little boys to feed and I married her and did my best to make her happy and see that she was taken care of. I took you and Joe in, too, Bill, and it wasn't easy marrying a woman with two little kids. I gave you a home and I did my best to be a father and a good husband.

"And damn it all, I know I'm not your dad. Never will be, couldn't ever be. But that's who you and your mother always wanted me to be. I'm not a cowboy, Bill. You know it and I know it. I make my living here in town. I teach music, for Gawd's sake. I play at weddings and dances and church socials. That's who I am and that's who I've always been. And I'm sorry I couldn't be more like your dad. He must have been one hell of a man.

"I tried to talk your mother out of goin' back out there on the desert and filing for that cussed homestead in Brown's Hole. But that's where she wants to be, Bill. She loves that life and I'm not a part of it. But in spite of all that, I still go there in the spring and help to plow and plant and brand and do all of that other farming and cowboy stuff. And I go out there in the fall and help put up the hay and wood and gather the steers and all. But that ranch is her place, Bill. I don't belong there and you know it. But, by Gawd, I've tried.

"And as far as beatin' you up as a kid. Yeah, I did that. But you had it comin'. You was always the most cantankerous damn kid. And you baited me, boy. You tormented me somethin' awful. You can't deny it. You know it's true.

"So go ahead, beat the hell out of me here in front of the whole town. I'm sure you can do it. But I ain't runnin', no matter what. You go ahead and do what you gotta do."

Bill stood there in his army shirt, his fists clenched, looking into the sad and pained eyes of his stepfather. The older man looked back over his own raised fists and his steady gaze never faltered. Bill looked around at the people gathered to watch. Like they had done to Winny Allred, no one would look back at him. They all turned their heads or looked at the ground, impassively. The only sound was the singing of birds in the nearby trees.

Finally, after what seemed like a long time, Bill put his hands down and turned to get his coat and hat. "I can't hit a pathetic guy like you, Winny. It wouldn't be sportin'."

"Shake my hand before you walk away!" came the challenge from behind him.

Bill turned in surprise to see his stepfather still standing there with his fists up in a classic Victorian boxing stance. "You shake my hand or don't you dare walk away from here," Winny threatened. "It ain't over unless we fight or shake hands."

Bill stood with his army coat over his arm and his hat in his hand, looking at the older man in bewilderment.

"By Gawd, I mean it, Bill. Don't you just walk away from here. You shake my hand or let's get this thing done. We ain't leavin' it like this."

Bill looked at the faces in the crowd. Some were looking back at him now and he could see disapproval and even anger in their eyes. His stepfather was right. Finish it now or forgive, forget, and forever let it be. He had called the man out in front of the whole town. He owed him at least that much.

Bill could see that the crowd was on his stepfather's side. He would have to leave town if he didn't do the right thing. If he walked away, the townspeople would never forgive him. He was caught in his own trap, there in front of all those people.

It took a while for the young soldier to muster the courage to swallow some of his pride. "Damn," he mumbled as he looked at the ground and dug the toe of his army boot in the dirt. He had to think it over for a moment. Everyone knew he could beat Winny Allred, but he just didn't have the heart to fight the man anymore. Everything his stepfather had said was true and Bill knew it. He was embarrassed and deeply ashamed for having called him out in public like that.

There was nothing else he could do. Bill took a deep breath and walked those long, lonely, and painful steps over to where his stepfather stood waiting. And then he held out his opened right hand. "I will shake hands with you, Winny. And I'm sorry about all of this."

"Good enough!" Winny said eagerly as he took Bill's hand in his best imitation of a rough cowboy handshake.

"I'll buy the beer," someone called from the edge of the crowd, and everyone started moving back toward the pool hall. A few of the men were patting their pal Winny Allred on the back while talking excitedly.

In just a few moments Bill found himself standing all alone in the middle of the street. He turned and started walking back toward his Grandma Moore's place. It was time to take off the uniform and put the war behind him. He had finally made peace with his troubled childhood. It was time to start a new life.

CHAPTER 7

MAKING A NEW START

BILL TIBBETTS AND EPHRAIM MOORE stepped down from their horses and stood looking south down the gaping canyons of the Green River channel. They were high on a rim in the land between the rivers, about twenty miles west of Moab.

"What do you think?" Ephraim said with a wry smile as he took off his hat and mopped his brow with an old red bandana. The July sun was hot and heat shimmers danced above the rocks, partly obscuring the 100-mile view down the river. The land before them was a tangle of deep canyons and high sandstone rims.

"Damn," Bill responded quietly, "It's rougher than I remember; hotter, too."

"Well, we ain't there yet." Ephraim said with another smile. "I'll bet the grass is taller than your stirrups down there someplace, and I don't think anyone else has been desperate enough to try to run cows in such a rough damn place."

"Well, I'm purdy desperate, all right," Bill said with a smile of his own. "I just hope these crowbait old horses of yours'll get us in and out of there. I'd sure hate to walk home."

"You better make friends with that cranky old pack mule then," Eph said smugly, trying not to smile. "If your mount gives out, you ain't gettin' mine."

Both men laughed, remounted their trusty steeds and turned north toward Mineral Canyon and the top of the Horsethief Trail. Bill was only kidding about the horses being crowbaits. Ephraim owned some good horses. He just felt bad that he had to borrow one. He didn't own a horse of his own yet and he would have to fix that soon.

The Horsethief Trail took them off the high mesa to the Green River. From there they set out to explore the country to the south.

OPPOSITE: *Uncle Eph and horse pack on Hardscrabble Hill*

For a couple of weeks Bill and Ephraim searched the rims and river bottoms south and west of Island in the Sky. They went forty or fifty miles down the river, checking the canyons and the ridges between the canyons, searching for grass and water. It was rough damn country, as Ephraim had suggested that it would be, with lots of sand and sandstone, scrub cedar, cactus and sage. They found no hidden valleys with thick carpets of grass like they had hoped for, but there was enough feed scattered in the rocks and on the hillsides to support a respectable herd if the cattle were spread over a wide area. And there was a little water there, too. The canyons had dry washes and not flowing steams of water, but there were a few springs in the sandy bottoms that could be developed and used. Most of the water was high in alkali content, but good enough for livestock. They found a few natural tanks in the slickrock that could be used by cattle, as well.

They found the country empty, but there were signs that someone had recently been there. There were a few old tracks suggesting that some stock, probably sheep, had been pastured there during the last winter. But there were no stockmen to challenge their right to be there, and no other man's cows eating the summer grass … as yet. As far as they could tell, they had found a virgin territory unclaimed by any of the big cow outfits.

Bill and Ephraim were excited. They hurried back to Moab to make their final plans. They would gather what stock they could from the White Rim and from Bill's mother's place to put together a herd to take to their new range as soon as possible. They had to take possession before another stockman moved in on the land they had found. But first, Bill had to buy some horses.

The dusty cowboys arrived back in Moab on the 23rd of July, just one day before the town's big Pioneer Day celebration. The 24th of July was the day the first Mormon pioneers had entered the Salt Lake Valley back in 1847, and every year the event was celebrated with religious zeal all over the state of Utah. The boys found Moab crowded with people and there was a carnival atmosphere on the streets. Tomorrow there would be a big parade down Main Street, a horse race or two, a baseball game, a picnic in the park and a big dance in the evening. It was the most celebrated holiday of the year and people were flocking to town from all over the area, wearing their Sunday best.

Bill's uncle, Will Moore, had come to town for a few days to enjoy the festivities, and Bill was excited. The young man hadn't seen his favorite uncle for a long time. More important than that, the older cowboy worked for one of the big cow outfits on the Book Cliffs and he might know where to get some good horses.

Everyone in Moab knew Will Moore. He was famous in eastern Utah because he had a wooden leg like a pirate. Most people knew him as "Peg Leg Moore." Actually, the leg was made of cork instead of wood, and it was only his foot and not his whole leg that was missing, but the man walked like a penguin in a stiff, shuffling gate that made him stand out in a crowd. When he went to town, little kids came running to get a good look at the big cowboy with the wooden stump for a leg.

Will had lost his leg in November 1905, while herding cows in the Dubinky Wash area, about twenty miles northwest of Moab. He was working for a man named Shorty Connell at the time. The ground was covered with snow and Will was chasing after a steer when his horse stepped in a badger hole while running full tilt. The horse broke its leg and came crashing down on top of Will, who was pinned beneath the animal with his foot twisted back and his toes pointed in the wrong direction. When the horse came down on his foot like that, it shattered Will's ankle and pushed a splinter of bone through the skin "several inches," according to the Moab newspaper.

Will was alone and had a terrible time getting out from under the injured horse. He would kick the animal in the face with his uninjured foot to make it rise up just a little, and each time he would try to pull the broken leg a little further out from under the floundering beast. The pain was terrible, but Will was finally able to pull the broken leg free. He shot the horse to put it out of its misery, and he might have considered doing himself the same favor, but he didn't.

The man was alone with the shattered leg, bleeding, in shock, on the ground and in the snow. He couldn't walk and there was nothing to ride. He was at least a mile from the cow camp and about fifteen miles from the nearest settlement at Courthouse Station. But, like the trooper he was, Will started to crawl on his hands and knees through the snow. He left a trail of blood and a strange furrow in the snow that was the drag mark of the broken bone sticking out through his torn boot. The cold and snow might have saved him from bleeding to death by helping the wound to clot.

Luckily, when Will didn't show up at the cow camp by late that afternoon, his boss, Shorty Connell, went looking for him and found him crawling in the snow toward camp. Will had lost a lot of blood and he was almost frozen to death. He had shot all of his bullets trying to attract someone's attention. Shorty took Will to camp and made him as comfortable as possible, then rode to Courthouse Station to summon help. Will had to stay all night in a tent without medication or anyone to attend to his needs or keep a fire going. It took eighteen hours for Shorty Connell to summon the doctor from Moab and return to the cold tent where Will was waiting.

Over the next two days, Dr. Williams treated the injured man while he was transported to Thompson Springs in an open buckboard. The rescue party took the shortest possible route, breaking

NOVEMBER 24, 1905

The Grand Valley Times

A DISTRESSING ACCIDENT

As the Times was about to go to print this Friday eve, word is received over the telephone from Court House that Will Moore had met with an accident about 15 miles west of Court House. Moore's horse fell with him crushing the bones of his right leg just above the ankle the bones coming through the flesh several inches, Shorty Connell, for whom Moore was working was either near or found Moore soon after. He had to leave the man alone and ride to Court House for help. Dr. Williams and Crip Taylor have gone. The probabilities are that the limb will have to be amputated, and it may be found advisable to go to railroad and to Salt Lake City. The nights are very cold and the suffering the man must undergo tonight alone in a helpless condition is appalling, and help cannot reach him much before day break.

DECEMBER 1, 1905

The Grand Valley Times

WILL MOORE'S FOOT AMPUTATED

Dr. Williams and party reached the scene of the accident to Will Moore reported in last weeks Times on Saturday noon and found Moore's condition such that amputation of the foot appeared necessary. The doctor accompanied Moore to Grand Junction hospital, reaching there Sunday night. The ride across the desert was tough and painful, as a long distance had to be made over a route where no wagon road existed. The Valley City camp was reached about 10 p.m. Saturday evening where they rested until next day and then went into Thompson in time to get the evening train into Grand Junction. Drs. Ball, Hansen, and Williams amputated the foot that night and Dr. Williams returned to Moab on Tuesday. He reports Moore doing as well as possible considering the nature of the accident.

trail through the rocks and sagebrush where no road existed. Buckboards were appropriately named. They had iron-rimmed wooden wheels mounted on axles that were bolted directly to the wagon box without any springs. The trip was absolute torture for a man with a compound fracture.

The rescue party and their patient stayed the first night at a place called Valley City, about twelve miles southwest of Thompson Springs. When they reached Thompson Springs on the afternoon of the second day, Will was put on a train and taken to a hospital in Grand Junction, Colorado, where his foot was amputated.

It was a bitter pill to lose a foot, but, as a tough and practical man like Will Moore might have said, his foot was a long ways from his heart, so things could have been worse. Just a few months later, Will was back to herding cows. He simply wired a tin can to his right stirrup, and with his stump tucked firmly in the can, it was hard to tell he was a one-legged cowboy—unless he got off his horse, of course.

In Moab, on the 24th of July 1919, Bill Tibbetts was happy to see his peg-legged uncle. After the usual handshakes, back slaps, and bear hugs, the men got down to business over a foaming brew at the Moab pool hall. Except for Uncle Ephraim, of course. Ephraim was a better Mormon than the other two and adhered more strictly to the church's ban on alcohol, coffee, tea, and tobacco.

"I'm goin' in the cow business with Eph and I need some good horses," Bill said as he leaned forward over his beer mug so Will could better hear him over the din of the holiday crowd in the pool hall. "I'm talkin' about all-day horses, sixty-mile horses, horses that can cross that desert and not give out. We're crossin' the river to the Laterite country over near Hanksville and we gotta have some good mounts."

"You got pockets full of money?" Will asked with an amused smile.

"No, I ain't got much, and you know it," Bill said, becoming somewhat impatient with the older man. "But I thought maybe you could help me out. You know, maybe you got connections with one of the big outfits and could help me swing a deal or somethin'."

"Actually, you came to the right man," Will said very business-like. "I do know where you can get some good horses. And they won't cost you all that much, either. I'm in good with a band of Utes up on the White River country near Vernal, and they got just what you need."

"Indian ponies? Are you out of your mind?"

"They might not look as dandy as some of the horses you high-classed cowboys are used to," Will said with a sarcastic, half-drunken smile. "But they're tougher than boiled owl and more sure-footed than mountain goats. And they can go all day without a drink of water, too. Those horses run wild in the Book Cliff country when they're colts, and there ain't a better animal anywhere for workin' the rough country."

"Aw, I don't know, Will. Most Indian ponies I ever saw were almost starved to death."

"Those Northern Utes don't keep runted ponies like some of the other Indian tribes," Will promised. "They raise some good horses over on the Uintah Reservation. You'll have to see 'em to believe it."

—————————

Bill, Ephraim, and Uncle Will left for the Book Cliffs just two days later. Before they started out, Will gave them a lesson in the art of trading with the Indians.

"Those Utes are slowly learnin' the value of the white man's money," he said. "But when they trade horses, they gotta get somethin' of substance to show they made a good trade. If you go there to trade and take only money, they're gonna want whole big handfuls of the stuff to make it look like they got a good deal. So what you do is buy goods before you go, and then trade the goods for the horses instead of dealin' in money. I know it sounds crazy, but that's how it works. Twenty dollars' worth of blankets and calico, tin-ware, sugar, coffee, and such, will buy you a good sixty-dollar horse. If you go there with only money, that Indian is gonna want a hundred greenbacks for that same sixty-dollar horse. That's how it works. You can pay twenty dollars in goods or a hundred dollars in cash for the same animal. It all depends on how you trade."

For his first venture in the art of Indian trading, Bill took one of Ephraim's pack mules loaded with about forty dollars' worth of trade goods.

A few miles from the town of Ouray, Will introduced Bill and Eph to his Ute friends and the Indians took them out to the horse pastures. Bill could see right off that Uncle Will had been right. The Utes had some fine looking horses. Bill was excited.

To the Indians, horse-trading was sport as well as economics, and Bill got caught up in the spirit of the thing. It was great fun. For most of the day he haggled, bargained, postured, and pouted. Will and Ephraim were greatly amused.

Finally, late in the afternoon, after softening up his trading opponents with a good campfire meal, hot coffee, and cigars, Bill traded his goods for three fine horses. The Indians were happy. Bill was happy, too.

Back in Moab, Bill gave one of the horses to his stepbrother, Kenny Allred. Ken was just a little kid who looked up to Bill and wanted to be just like him. Bill promised to help Kenny be a

Book Cliffs Mesa

cowboy when he grew up, just like his uncles Will and Ephraim had done for him when he was a kid. The gift horse was a pinto, a fine looking animal with black and white spots that any Indian or aspiring young cowboy would be proud to ride. That fancy horse made Kenny Allred the most envied kid in Moab.

Bill's favorite horse to come out of his Indian trading adventure was a big bay gelding he named Ute. The big horse was the toughest and most reliable cowpony Bill Tibbetts ever owned, and he was a pleasure to ride. The Indians had trained old Ute, and like all good Indian horses, he could be mounted from either side, unlike most cowboy mounts that could only be approached from the left. The horse could also be guided Indian style by the rider's knees without the use of a bridle, and he had been taught impeccable manners. He didn't kick, he didn't bite, and he stood still while a man climbed aboard.

Bill and Ute developed a special bond of trust and confidence in one another. Ute would go wherever Bill pointed him, and Bill always took care of the horse's needs before his own. The two would spend many years and many thousands of miles together on the deserts and cattle ranges of southeastern Utah. Bill talked fondly about old Ute for the rest of his life. There was no other horse quite like him.

The young man took the rest of his savings and bought a few cows. It was a meager start for an ambitious young rancher, but it was the best he could do at the time. He also took Ute over to Brown's Hole and gathered all of his mother's cows he could find. Eph gathered most of his cows on the White Rim and bought a few more from some people from Texas who were selling out and going home. When Bill and Eph were ready and the pack mules loaded, they began their cattle drive to their new range on the Laterite country to the south. Elaterite Basin was the proper name of the place, but the Moab boys usually dropped the "E" and pronounced the name as "Laterite."

<hr>

It was fall when they reached Elaterite Basin with the cows. The cottonwoods were yellow and the sun was dropping lower to the south with each passing day. The nights were cold but the days still pleasantly warm in the shelter of the ledges.

They were scattering their cows in the grassy pockets among the rocks and rims, preparing to settle in for the winter, when they came upon another man's cow camp. They were surprised and very disappointed to find it. There might be trouble if another outfit was claiming the range. They stopped and checked their guns, just in case. They never knew who or what situation they might be riding into out in the wilderness like that. The sheriff and the lawyers were a long, long ways away.

The enemy camp was at the north end of Waterhole Flat, a little south of Elaterite Basin. As Bill and Ephraim approached, they could see several horses tied to pinyon trees near a couple of big tents. Small groups of cattle were grazing in the background. As they got closer, they could see men standing around a campfire while another man was poking inside a big Dutch oven with a long, wooden spoon.

Cautiously, Bill and Ephraim rode toward the camp. Ephraim was the older man so he did all of the talking. From near 100 yards out, he shouted, "Hello there, we are entering your camp. We come as friends."

The cowboys gathered around the campfire were surprised to see the men from Moab, but they were true to the Western code of hospitality and invited them down for beans, cornbread, and coffee. Everyone was impeccably polite, but tension hung heavy in the air. There were six or eight cowboys in the camp, but most of them were teenaged boys.

The boss of the outfit came out of a tent when summoned, and extended his hand cautiously in a sign of friendship. "My name is Lou Chaffin," he said. "We're from over by Torrey. Got a place on the Fremont River." He was a man in his mid-forties, a reformed gold miner making a new start in the cattle business. Chaffin knew the area well, much better than Bill and Ephraim. He had placer-mined for gold on the Colorado River for years and had crossed this country many times before.

At first the boys from Moab didn't quite know what to make of this intrusion on their new-found grazing land. But Mr. Chaffin had a good eye and he was civil. Things could have been much worse. It surprised them that the man was willing to shake hands and offer part of his own supper to a couple of rivals from across the river. It was a hopeful beginning. Bill and Ephraim introduced themselves and then sat at the other man's fire and shared his evening meal.

"We thought we was goin' to be all alone down here this winter," Ephraim said as he chewed on a chunk of overcooked cornbread.

"Us, too," Lou Chaffin offered. "We didn't expect anybody to be here, other than those French sheepmen, maybe. They come here under the ledge almost every winter now. It's a good place to winter sheep. They take those woolies back on the mountains in the spring. It gives the grass all summer to grow back, like it is now."

"Under the what?" Ephraim asked.

"Under the ledge," Chaffin answered, somewhat surprised. "That's where we are now. Under the Ledge."

"I thought this was the Laterite country," Ephraim said.

"It's called Elaterite Basin just north of here," Chaffin explained, "but it's all Under the Ledge. That's the ledge over there," he said, pointing to the towering shadow of the Orange Cliffs to the west.

The Orange Cliffs, also known as The Big Ledge, span almost forty miles along the western edge of the Green River basin. Near Elaterite Basin, The Big Ledge is over 1000 feet high and an intimidating barrier to travelers.

"Well, maybe you men from Torrey came down under that ledge, but me and Bill here, we crossed the river from Moab. We ain't come down under that ledge yet. I think we'll just keep callin' it the Laterite country."

"That makes a good point," Chaffin admitted, careful not to smile, afraid the other man might take offense.

"So how we gonna split this range?" Ephraim asked, getting down to business. "We got a herd just north of here, in that E-Laterite basin you talked about."

"Well, since we're both new here, and neither of us seems to have a prior claim, I guess it's up to us how we divide the grass," Chaffin said.

There was silence around the campfire for a while, and then Chaffin spoke. "Tell you what, since you men are already in the Big Water Wash country over in Elaterite, I'll keep my cows south of here in Waterhole Flat. We'll let this area here be our buffer for now. You keep your stock north of here and I'll keep my stock south of here. Does that sound fair enough?"

"How does that sound to you, Bill?" Ephraim asked.

"Sounds good to me."

Elaterite Basin with Orange Cliffs in background

Ephraim extended his hand toward Chaffin for a handshake. "You got a deal, Mr. Chaffin. We'll keep our stock in the Laterite country."

On the way back to their own camp in the chilly moonlight, Bill turned to Ephraim with a smile. "You cut a good deal with that man, Eph. We got half the range and we ain't got enough cows to fill half of what we got."

"That man don't know how many cows we've got," Ephraim grinned.

"And we don't know how many cows he has, either," Bill admitted.

"Yeah, but we'll find out. And so will he. The important thing is, we got us a first-user's right to run cows on this range. We got us a gentleman's agreement with our neighbor, and we'll fight anyone else who comes along. It looks like we're in the cattle business, nephew. How does it feel to be a man of substance?"

Bill on the Green River carrying supplies

CHAPTER 8

COWBOY LIFE ALONG THE RIVER

ILL AND EPHRAIM SPENT THE WINTER OF 1919-1920 in the Laterite country, camping out in a tent. They tended the cows and explored their new rangeland, digging out the springs and rough-fencing the water sources to prevent the cows from stomping them out. They also developed their trail between Moab and Elaterite Basin.

From Moab, Bill and Ephraim rode up Seven Mile Canyon to the Big Flat. There, they took the Horsethief Trail down Mineral Canyon to the Green River. Then they rode down the east side of the river about twelve miles to a place called Queen Anne Bottom. There was a wide, gravely ford at Queen Anne Bottom, and for most of the year they could cross the river there without swimming the horses. On the west bank of the river, across from Queen Anne Bottom, the cowboys followed the north fork of Horse Canyon away from the river and into Elaterite Basin.

Each of the small valleys or "bottoms" along the Green River channel had a name. Places like Tidwell Bottom, Anderson Bottom, and Valentine Bottom were named after families who had attempted homesteads there in the early 1900s. Places like Potato Bottom, Tent Bottom, and Turks Head Bottom were named after abandoned fields, abandoned equipment, and geologic features.

Queen Anne Bottom was probably named after Queen Ann Bassett (Ann without an "e") who was a good friend of Butch Cassidy and The Wild Bunch. Ann Bassett was a member of a prominent ranching family in the Brown's Park area of northwestern Colorado. She was one of the few women allowed to spend time with the outlaws in the Robbers Roost during the 1890s.

The new country Bill and Eph explored was surrounded by some of the world's most spectacular scenery, and one of the most impressive areas was a place the cowboys called "The Maze." It was an impossible tangle of deep, sandstone-finned canyons that stretched for several miles between Elaterite Basin and the river channel. The cowboys were aware of the beauty of the place, but they didn't go there often. It was a bad place to loose a cow. In 1919, only a handful of Anglo-Americans had ever seen the place. The rest of the world had no clue it even existed.

Elaterite Basin was terribly remote. There were no developed roads. Everything had to be taken in with mules or packhorses. The French sheepmen had pioneered what they called The Flint Trail. It was a steep and rocky pack trail that traversed The Big Ledge to the west, and it was the best trail to Hanksville or the town of Green River. There was a North Trail out of Elaterite, too. It went over North Point toward Hans Flat and the Robbers Roost country. But Bill and Ephraim were from Moab and they preferred to do their shopping there. When they went to Moab for supplies, they had the river crossing at Queen Anne Bottom and their new trail along the river all to themselves.

The Green River was a special challenge for the cowboys. There were no dams upstream to regulate the flow of water and the river ran wild and free. The water level fluctuated constantly, depending on the weather and time of year. Floods were common and river crossings were dangerous. Bill and Ephraim kept extra horses and caches of riding equipment, saddles, and other supplies on both sides of the river so they could cross back and forth on rafts when the water was high and dangerous. When they made a raft, they would spread a canvas tarp over the top of the raft to keep water from splashing up between the logs and wetting the cargo. The rafts were guided with long, cottonwood poles.

But the cowboys preferred to ride or swim their horses across the river if they could. It was easier, faster, and less bother than making a raft, even if they did get wet in the process.

Bill and Ephraim were riding through Potato Bottom one fine summer morning when Ephraim said he had been looking at a spot on the river that he thought might be shallow enough to ford without swimming. Since the weather was warm and the water was low, he thought it might be a good time to check it out. As Bill watched, Ephraim got down from his horse and cut a stout cottonwood sapling, about twelve feet long, to use as a "sounding rod" to test the depth of the river. He then rode to the edge of the water and sat watching the current.

"Looks too deep to me," Bill declared.

"I don't think it's that bad," Eph proclaimed. "I think me and ol' Sugarfoot here can walk on across."

"Sugarfoot ain't that tall," Bill insisted. "You better build a raft or give it up. That river has swallowed better swimmers than you and that old red horse."

"We can do it," Eph insisted, as he turned the horse down the bank and into the water.

Bill sat and watched as Ephraim went farther and farther out into the current. The water came higher and higher up Eph's leg toward his saddlebags and coiled rope. The man was going along slowly, cautiously sounding the bottom with his long, cottonwood pole.

Then, in slow motion, the big horse simply dropped out of sight beneath the waves. Then Eph went under, still sitting in the saddle. The long pole went slowly down and out of sight, and there wasn't a riffle or a bubble to be seen while Bill watched anxiously, holding his breath.

Finally, the long pole came rocketing up out of the water like a cork, followed by Ephraim, blowing like a whale. Then came the wild-eyed horse, swimming for all he was worth. Horses are good swimmers, but Eph beat that horse to the far shore, cowboy boots and all. They crossed the river somewhere else after that.

————•+•————

During one of the winters in the early 1920s, the Green and Colorado rivers froze solid. In Moab, Bill nailed corked shoes on old Ute and his packhorses and was able to ride on the ice down the Colorado and up the Green River all the way to Anderson Bottom. The journey was about sixty miles following the contours of the rivers, and the ice made a smooth, flat road. The weather was cold but it was the fastest, easiest, and most pleasant trip to the cow camps Bill had ever experienced. The only trouble was, once in a while the ice would crack with a sound like a rifle shot and it would scare the hell out of him and the horses.

When all of that ice broke up in the spring, the noise was terrible, sounding like cannon fire in the canyons, and it kept the cowboys awake for several nights. Masses of ice dammed the river near Anderson Bottom and flooded most of the low-lying areas. When the ice dam collapsed, huge blocks of ice pushed down the river, spilling over the banks and ripping out willows and cottonwood trees like giant bulldozers. Having no news or contact with anyone outside of the river canyons, Bill wondered if the whole world wasn't in the beginning stages of a new ice age.

————•+•————

Through the early 1920s, Elaterite Basin became the core area for the Moore, Tibbetts, and Allred cattle operation. Bill and Ephraim ran several hundred head of cattle there and along the river bottoms as far north as Mineral Canyon. They maintained control of Ephraim's range on the White Rim above the river, as well. Their operation was spread for more than forty miles along that narrow strip of river and they held the outfit together with sweat, determination, and miles in the saddle.

They never did build a cabin in Elaterite, preferring to remain mobile and follow the cattle with just a bedroll and a light camp outfit. Stockmen of the day called it "laying out" with the cattle. Being able to stay with the herd gave them an advantage in the cow business. Their losses to the elements, quicksand, rustlers, and predators were less than most of their neighbors.

However, it was still necessary to go to town for supplies, and it was a long trek. Most often, only one of them would go to town while the other stayed and watched over the herd. A quick trip to Moab and back to Elaterite would usually take eight to ten days, depending on the time of year and such variables as weather, the flow of the river, and what business needed to be taken care of in town.

On one of those early springtime supply runs, Ephraim told Bill that he would be back in two weeks, but he never showed up. After waiting for a month, Bill was out of grub and down to shooting rabbits for his supper. He worried that something terrible must have happened to Ephraim, and he decided to ride to town to find out.

Bill was camped on the west side of the river near Anderson Bottom, and the river was high with spring runoff. Instead of swimming old Ute across the river, he turned the horse loose and made a raft of cottonwood logs to ferry himself across. On the east side, he got a saddle and riding gear from a cache near one of his old cowboy camps. There, too, he was able to catch an old gray gelding belonging to Uncle Ephraim. The gray horse hadn't been used for quite some time and he was fat and lazy. When Bill stepped into the stirrup, the horse exploded in a squealing, snorting, bucking-horse fit.

Bill was a good cowboy and he hung in there, but the horse took him down through a jungle of greasewoods, tall willows, and cottonwood saplings along the river bottom where the tangled brush and thorns tore Bill's clothes to shreds and cut him up pretty good. But in spite of the beating he suffered from the brush, Bill rode the horse until it gave out and quit bucking. He couldn't let the horse throw him and escape with the saddle. He also knew it was a long ways to town, and no self-respecting cowboy would ever walk to town and admit that he had been bucked off and abandoned by his stupid horse. He would be laughed at forever.

After subduing the horse, Bill was covered with bruises and bloodied with dozens of cuts and scrapes from the willows and greasewood thorns. To complicate matters, his shirt and jeans were ripped to tatters and he didn't have a change of clothes. Luckily, there was another man's cow camp between him and Moab. He decided to stop there and see if he could borrow a shirt and a pair of Levis.

Loren Taylor was still sleeping the next morning when Bill threw open the tent flap and loudly announced his presence. "Get up and pee, Loren! The world's on fire!"

The sleep-groggy young man sat up in his bedroll and was nearly scared out of his wits to see a wild man standing in the doorway of his tent. The wild man was nearly naked and his body was covered with cuts and bruises. The unrecognized whiskered face was scraped and bruised and the eyes were almost swollen shut.

With a scream, the young cowboy dove for the back of the tent and started digging like a prairie dog to get out from under the tent skirt. Bill caught him by the foot and dragged him back, squealing like a pig. Loren was wearing only his long underwear and Bill was laughing so hard he could hardly talk, but he tried to calm his panicked friend. "Hold on there, pardner, it's me, Bill Tibbetts. Don't you recognize me, for Pete's sake? ...I need yer help, Loren. Quit kickin' and listen to me for a minute..." It took some fast-talking to convince the man to settle down and stop kicking.

Finally, the hypertensive Loren calmed down a little and found his voice. Still breathing heavily, and with his face flushed with embarrassment, he said, "Damn you, Bill. I thought you was the devil for sure. What happened to you? You look like you been through a corn chopper. Where's your clothes?"

"Little accident with a bad horse," Bill said as he helped Loren to his feet.

"You ever tell anyone about this, I'll knock the shit out of you," Loren warned.

"I'd buy a ticket to see that," Bill grinned, reaching out to further mess up the young man's hair.

The boys had a good laugh, and then Bill asked for a change of clothes. Unfortunately, Loren didn't have any extras. However, he did tell Bill about an abandoned cow camp over on the rim where he (Loren) had thrown away an old pair of worn-out Levis the winter before.

Bill rode the bad-tempered gray horse over there and found the discards. They were sun-bleached, rotten, and filled with sand. The knees and the seat were threadbare and worn through, but they were better than nothing, and nothing was the only alternative. Bill shook the sand and spiders out and put them on. They didn't fit worth a darn, and they made him itch like crazy, but at least they covered his private parts ... some. They were too tight in the waist to button and the legs ended way above his ankles.

Bill tried to reach Moab while it was still dark, but morning overtook him at the bottom of Moab Canyon. As he crossed the river bridge he could see people coming from town and he recognized a pretty girl he knew and her mother riding in a buggy. Not wearing a shirt and not wanting to be seen in his rotting, castoff Levis, he quickly turned his horse into a little cove where the road forked at a place called Matrimony Springs.

As luck would have it, the pretty girl and her mother turned that way, too. They drove the carriage right past the bare and blushing young cowboy. The women looked right at him, then turned their noses up in disgust and continued on their way, pretending they hadn't seen the scantily dressed young saddle tramp. Proper and respectable ladies would never speak to such a bum. With delight, Bill realized they hadn't recognized him with his long hair, winter whiskers, and scratched and swollen face.

Whistling a happy tune, the bare and beat-up young cowboy continued on into Moab. On the way, he passed his brother Joe, and Joe didn't recognize him either. Under the circumstances, Bill decided that being unrecognized was better cover than a shirt. He stopped at his grandma's place, washed up, shaved, and dressed himself in a proper set of clothes.

An hour later, he found Ephraim down in the fields, on a ladder, happily pruning the fruit trees.

"What are you doin'?" Bill challenged with righteous indignation. "I darn near starved to death waitin' for you to come back with the groceries. I had to raft the river, buck-out ol' Blue in the greasewoods, and ride halfway to hell just to find you prunin' the fruit trees? I though you was dead, or stranded on the desert with a broken leg or somethin'."

"Sorry about that," Eph said sheepishly. "There was lots of chores to do here around the place and time just got away from me. What happened to you, Bill? You look like you been run over by a train."

"Old Blue is in the corral," Bill said with an evil eye. "You want to take him to the livestock sale, or you want me to shoot him?"

"Enough said," Ephraim smiled. "Darn, I wish I'd been there to see it."

"Shut up," Bill said. And then he walked away.

A day or two later, Bill asked that pretty and proper young lady for a date. He took her to an ice cream social. With his new haircut, shave, and clean shirt, she never suspected she was holding hands with the saddle tramp she had encountered along the river. When she asked about the scratches on his face and his swollen eyes, he fed her a long story about wrestling mountain lions to protect the cow camp. She knew it was a tall tale, but enjoyed the story just the same. There was something delightful about a handsome young cowboy with mysterious wounds.

———•◦•———

Bill got his turn to go to town for supplies, too. On one of those trips, he was returning to Elaterite Basin with his packsaddles loaded when he reached a familiar old camping spot after dark. There was a fine water hole there. The young cowboy unsaddled his horse and pack animals, hobbled them, and turned them loose to graze. He then lit a fire, made a camp, and settled in to get some supper. Dipping his water bucket in the pond, he went back to his camp to make coffee and Dutch oven biscuits by the light of the fire.

As he sat by the campfire eating his evening meal, he was annoyed to find several strands of hair in the biscuits. He decided that he'd have to be more careful when cooking around the horse gear and saddle blankets from then on.

The next morning, when the sun came up, he found a big, bloated, and very dead horse floating in the water hole. It had been there so long the hair was slipping from the rotting carcass and floating on top of the water. His water bucket was full of putrid horsehair.

When Bill reached Elaterite and found Uncle Ephraim, he told the old cowboy all about it.

"What did you do?" Eph asked with a shudder.

"What could I do?" Bill said with an innocent face. "I discovered a whole new way to make biscuits. I gathered up a bunch of that horsehair and put it in the flour sack. Makes them biscuits hold together real good. Helps 'em stick to yer ribs, too."

"Damn you. If you put that stinkin' horsehair in the flour you'll have to eat it all."

"That's what I figured," Bill said with an impish grin. "I put horsehair in the sugar, molasses, and raisins, too," he teased. "You better stay out of those things, Eph. Wouldn't want you to get horsehair fever. I'm immune, ya know. I got inoculated at the dead horse waterhole."

———•◦•———

Illness, accidents, and rattlesnakes were other concerns when town and the doctors were fifty miles away. Bill had a close call during the winter of 1921.

The cowboys made a winter camp in a large rock shelter in Potato Bottom. Bill was sleeping one night with his bedroll spread out near the fire when something bit him on the lip. He jumped up and pulled a small gray scorpion off his face. His mouth was numb for a while, but he managed to go back to sleep.

In the morning his lip was swollen to several times its normal size. His whole face was puffy and his mouth burned like fire. His throat was swollen, too, and it was hard for him to swallow. In his shaving mirror, he discovered the lip was an ugly blue-black color, and he decided he had better ride to Moab and have the doctor check it out.

The first day he rode to the top of the rim near Island in the Sky. He stayed there that night, camping out in the junipers. That night it snowed eighteen inches, and by morning the whole world was filled with fog. Bill couldn't see but a few yards in the soupy mist, but he started for Moab anyway, trusting his instincts to find his way.

Several hours later, when he stumbled upon the remains of his camp from the night before, he realized that he had been riding in circles and had lost his way. He had no choice but to stop and wait for the sky to clear.

For days he waited, alone and in great pain from his infected lip. The weather was frigid and the trees frosted with ice that never melted in the cold, damp fog. He spent days and nights sitting by a smoky campfire, low on food and low in spirit, nursing his throbbing, wounded mouth. It was almost a week before the fog cleared and Bill could get his bearings from the sun and the mountains again. He made his way to Moab where Doc Allen lanced his scorpion wound and drained a great deal of fluid from the abscess. There were no antibiotics in the 1920s, but Bill healed quickly. He hung around town for a few days while his swollen face returned to something closer to normal, and then he headed for the cattle ranges again.

In the course of events, Bill teamed up with his cousin, Tom Perkins, to run a trap line along the river. Cousin Tom was ten years older than Bill, but he was single, footloose, and fancy-free. He loved the desert and his bachelor lifestyle.

Bill and Tom got along very well. Bill was a natural leader and Tom was a natural follower. Tom was a man of sound mind and character, but low on ambition and material wealth. It didn't take much to make him happy. Tom saw no reason to work long hours in an office, a mine, or a hayfield. The few dollars he made with his traps and his rifle fulfilled his meager needs. With no family to feed and no property to maintain, camping out on the desert suited him just fine.

Yet, in spite of his laid-back nature, Tom was a true daredevil, one of the few people who could keep up with Bill Tibbetts when Bill decided to do something wild and crazy. Tom admired Bill and was always entertained by the younger man's energy, rowdy imagination, and devil-may-care attitude.

Along the river bottoms, the boys would tend Bill's cows, and in the course of their travels they would set traps for anything they could catch: beaver, coyotes, bobcats, cougars, and foxes. The furs brought a decent price and there was the additional incentive of bounties paid by stockmen's associations and county governments for wolves, coyotes, and cats. Wolves had pretty well been eradicated by then, but there were still a few. The boys were good at trapping and they did well.

Bill and Tom claimed Anderson Bottom as the base camp for their trapping operation, but

Uncle Eph at Turks Head on the Green River

they made a log cabin at Turk's Head Bottom, a few miles downstream from there, too. Bill owned a .44 revolver that he packed on his saddle. He practiced with it often and was considered to be a pretty good shot. At night after the boys got into their bedrolls in the cabin, he would put the candle out by shooting the flame off the wick. He got a few packrats and spiders while shooting from his bed, too. Bill slept with the gun tucked under his bedroll where it would be handy in the dark of night. A man never knew who or what might come calling in the moonlight.

One late-winter afternoon, Bill and Tom Perkins were riding into Anderson Bottom toward their camp. The sun was dropping behind the western rim and the sky was on fire. They had been checking traps and their saddles were adorned with furs, traps, and firearms.

They were almost in sight of their camp when Tom pulled up his horse and held his hand out for Bill to stop. He sat there for a moment with a puzzled look on his face, and then he said, "Good Lord, Bill. What's that awful smell?"

"Smells like sheep," Bill said with his nose in the air. "It sure does. It smells like sheep."

The boys continued around a bend in the trail, and there, sure enough, were fifty or sixty sheep. The woolies were nibbling happily at the bushes and chomping down on the grass. Behind those they could see a whole lot more. Sheep were scattered all across the hillside above their camp and hundreds more dotted the landscape for as far as they could see.

"Damn!" Bill cussed. "Those Frenchmen have been runnin' sheep over under the ledge for several winters now, but there ain't supposed to be any sheep here along the river. This is our range, damn it."

"Looks like a million of them," Tom said with some alarm. "There won't be enough grass left to feed a rabbit if they stick around for more than a day or two. Those sheep eat everything right down to the roots."

"Well, we're gonna help this herd keep moving," Bill said with real conviction. "I ain't puttin' up with this. Let's go find that herder and tell him to get the flock outta here. We got the grazing rights to this river bottom and we're not giving it up."

But it was getting dark and they couldn't find a herder anywhere.

"Don't they bunch sheep at night to keep the coyotes and wolves away?" Tom asked.

"Most sheepmen do," Bill agreed. "But this herd is so big and scattered so far, there probably ain't enough sheepherders in the whole country to gather this bunch."

"So, what we gonna do?" Tom asked.

"Well, I guess we'll have to wait until morning to do anything," Bill said. "But since those woolies are eatin' our grass tonight, I think it's only fair that we have mutton for supper. What do you think?"

"You wouldn't dare," Tom grinned.

Bill took his coiled rope from his saddle and rode over to the nearest little bunch of sheep. The light was fading fast, but he picked out a young one and threw the rope. He dragged the big lamb over to their camp, killed, skinned, and butchered it while Tom took care of the horses, kindled a fire and made coffee. A short time later they kicked back to enjoy a well-deserved feast of lamb chops and Dutch oven biscuits.

"Kinda greasy, ain't it?" Tom suggested, not meaning to complain, but just stating a fact. "This meat's a lot different than eating beef or deer."

"You gotta eat it hot," Bill grinned. "You let it cool and that sheep tallow sticks to the roof of your mouth."

"I don't think I like eatin' sheep much," Tom decided.

"That's why an old coyote will sit out on a hill in the evening and lick his ass," Bill said with a big smile. "He's tryin' to get the taste of those sheep outta his mouth."

Early the next morning, just at daylight, Bill was awakened by the sound of footsteps near the tent. He peeked out from under the flap of the tent and saw a pair of boots just a few feet away. Grabbing his .44 from under his bedroll, he took a quick aim and blasted dirt all over the boots. Jumping up, he ran to the door of the tent and shot two or three more times into the dirt and into the air. He yelled for the herders to get the hell out of there and take those stinkin' damn sheep with them. By that afternoon the sheep were gone.

"You didn't shoot that man, did you, Bill?"

"I don't think so. I was just tryin' to help him move those sheep along. A man's got to protect what's rightfully his."

A few days later, Uncle Ephraim came riding into the camp at Anderson Bottom. He was leading a string of packhorses loaded down with panniers stuffed with oats, food, and camp supplies. He had been in Moab for a few weeks and was coming back to take over the cow operation to give Bill and Tom a chance to go to town.

But when Eph rode into camp he wasn't smiling or cracking any jokes. Bill and Tom could tell right off that something wasn't right. The boys stood by anxiously and waited for the man to speak.

Ephraim stepped down from his horse, turned his back to the boys, and began undoing the cinch on his saddle. Then, very matter-of-fact, he asked over his shoulder, "Are you the guys who shot that sheepherder?"

Tom turned toward Bill with real concern in his eyes. Bill stood his ground, stoic as an Indian, and didn't say anything.

"Somebody shot a sheepherder a few days ago," Eph said as he pulled his saddle from the horse. "At least that's the word around town. Rumor has it there's a warrant for the arrest of the man who did it."

"Do they know who did it?" Bill asked with a wrinkled brow, beginning to show signs of nervous concern.

"No," Eph said. "The herder didn't get a look at the guy, but they say it happened at Anderson Bottom. You fellers know anyone who might have been camped in Anderson Bottom the past week or so?"

"Aw, damn it all, Eph. I didn't shoot that sheepherder. I only shot near his feet. I needed to give him a reason to move those mountain maggots outta here. There were millions of 'em and they were eatin' everything right down to the dirt."

"Well, the rumor is, that sheepman was shot. True, he wasn't hurt bad, but shooting sheepherders is against the law, even if you only wing one. You boys better pack your gear and get the hell outta here. I'd go over in Laterite and lay low for a month or two if it was me. I just come from town so they know I didn't do it. I'll take over your camp here to cover your tracks."

"Probably peppered him with gravel," Bill decided, thinking it over. "I did shoot purdy close to his feet. But I didn't shoot the guy. That .44 would have took his foot off."

"I didn't hear any calls in town for a posse," Eph continued. "But I wouldn't be surprised if the sheriff ain't here in a day or so to check things out."

The boys went to work gathering up their gear.

"I'll bet the trappin' is real good over in Laterite," Tom said hopefully as he rolled up his bedroll.

"Yeah, I'll bet you're right," Bill agreed as he stuffed his army mess kit into a saddlebag. "We better go over there and check it out. Who knows, maybe we'll stay all summer."

"Take two of those packhorses with you," Eph offered. "They're packin' enough grub and horse feed to get you by for a month or so. I'll let you know when the dust settles around here and the coast is clear."

Bill and Tom hurried down the river, into the wilds of Elaterite Basin and the land under the ledge. They stayed there for a few months, lying low and waiting for word from Ephraim about the sheriff. While there, they trapped for the rest of the season and worked the Moore, Tibbetts, and Allred cattle.

The boys laughed about their new status as wanted desperados, but it just didn't seem right that they were in so much trouble. Making a sheepherder dance to the tune of a .44-Special was sport and not criminal assault, at least the way they saw it. And besides, Bill was defending his territory. Those sheepmen should expect to be shot when they moved in on a cowman like that.

Around the campfire at night, Bill smiled when telling Tom how those sheepherders sure could dance when they put their mind to it. And Tom grumbled that if he was going to be arrested for the incident, it was sure too bad he didn't get to see it happen. He'd never seen a sheepman do the high-step before. The boys laughed about it, but they were very cautious about strangers and they kept a close eye on their back-trail, just in case.

The sheriff never showed up. Some people in Moab suspected that Bill and Tom had done the shooting, but a warrant for their arrest was never served. Probably, the sheriff knew that if the sheepman couldn't identify the gunman, the effort to arrest and try the boys in a court would be futile. The savvy lawman chalked it up as one more incident in the continuing mini-range wars plaguing the whole territory. The injured sheepman left town quietly, none the worse for wear, and the incident was soon forgotten.

CHAPTER 9

DROUGHT, INDIAN TROUBLE, AND MURDER

HERE WAS A TIME IN EASTERN UTAH WHEN rain fell often and the grass grew thick and tall. From the time of the earliest settlers in the Moab area, in the late 1870s, to about 1920, the land was blessed. Pioneers and early stockmen told of grass up to their horses' stirrups and clear water flowing where none is found today. In those years people dry-farmed the Cisco desert and the river bottoms of the Green and Colorado.

People called it a desert back then, but it was a different desert from what we know today. It was a green and prosperous desert. Deer, antelope, desert bighorn sheep, and wild horses roamed the backcountry and there were willows and cottonwoods along every small watercourse. It was a boom time for the stock industry, and dozens of small towns and ranches dotted the landscape.

Then the rain stopped and the country dried up. It didn't happen overnight. The climate change came on slowly, little by little and year by year. Every year there was a little less rain and a little less grass. It took a long time for people to understand that the wet years had been an anomaly.

The farmers, ranchers, and sheepmen fought back as best they could, but in the end, dry farms failed, small streams became dry gulches, water wells dried up, and many ranches, homesteads, and little towns had to be abandoned. By the mid-1920s, places like Cisco, Marrs, Danish Flat, Woodside, and Valley City were melting back into the sand. Eastern Utah got an early start on the "dust bowl" years of the 1930s.

The good times had brought tens of thousands of cattle and sheep to the area and they were still there when the rain stopped. With less grass for the same numbers of livestock, the range was soon overgrazed and competition for grass and water became intense. Disputes were inevitable and there was much contention on the stock ranges. The situation was made worse by a lack of laws governing grazing rights and public use of public lands.

Elaterite Basin was hit especially hard. It was a marginal range for livestock in the best of years, and during a prolonged drought it became untenable. In 1923, the grass was short and stunted for want of rain. The blades of green were withered, dry, and parched like straw in the merciless sun. Most of the seep springs went dry and the slickrock water tanks were filling with blow sand. The cattle had to range farther and farther to find water and feed. The miles, heat, and lack of proper sustenance took their toll on the herd. The cows were thin and foot-weary from the constant searching for water and grass.

<hr />

They met on a rough and narrow trail, high above the river. Bill was going north with his pack-saddles empty, headed for town. Ephraim was headed south with his packsaddles loaded, going to Elaterite. They hadn't seen each other for a few weeks so they got down from the horses to talk. The horses were happy to take a rest. The late-July sun was drawing copious amounts of horse sweat and the red rocks beneath their feet were scorched like toast. Eph's packhorses, especially, took full advantage of the rest stop, leaning from side to side to give one leg at a time a little relief from the heavy loads they were carrying.

"How's it looking over in Laterite?" Eph asked, hopefully. But he already knew the answer.

"Gawdawful dry," Bill replied, taking his hat off to give his sweat-soaked hair a taste of cool air. "We're runnin' out of feed over there real fast, Eph. If we don't get rain soon we're gonna be in big trouble."

"It's the same all the way up the river, too," Eph replied. "I've never seen it this dry or this hot. I don't know what we're gonna do this winter if the grass don't grow. We can't teach these cows to eat sand."

"What's it like up on top?" Bill asked, referring to the canyon rims near Island in the Sky. The elevation was much higher there and the area always got more rain and snow than the river bottoms.

"There's a little grass up there in the Big Flat country, but not as much as normal. I've never seen the White Rim this bad either. If it don't rain soon we might have to sell out. I don't know what else to do. Better to sell than watch 'em all winter kill."

"Let's not give up too soon, Uncle," Bill scolded. "We've worked too hard to sell out. If we have to, I'll hire some Navajo to do a rain dance for us. That ought to do the trick. And besides, I've got a black cloud that seems to follow me around everywhere. Maybe that cloud will bring us some rain. Let's give it another month or two before we talk about sellin' out."

"Yeah, I guess you're right," Eph agreed. "But if the grass don't get to growin' purdy quick, we've got a big decision to make, 'long about October."

"It'll all work out," Bill promised.

"Yeah, I guess so."

"So, how we gonna get past each other on this darn narrow trail?"

"I guess you'll have to back your horses up," Eph said with his best poker-faced smile. "My pack saddles are full and I'm not turnin' around."

There was Indian trouble that year, too. The year 1923 saw the last "Indian war" ever to be fought on American soil. Again, it happened in Utah's San Juan County, and like the Indian war of 1915, the whole thing was an unnecessary tragedy.

Early that year, San Juan County Sheriff William Oliver arrested two young Utes for robbing a sheep camp, killing a calf, and burning a bridge. The part about robbing the sheep camp and burning the bridge suggested the Indians might have been guilty of thievery and criminal mischief. The part about killing a calf indicated they were hungry. The ancient Ute hunting and gathering way of life was effectively dead by the 1920s, but the Utes themselves were still alive. And they were caught in a time warp. Their material culture, language, worldview, mindset, religion, oral history, social organization, moral codes, and mitochondrial DNA were still rooted in that older time. The Utes were lost and starving in the modern world.

The two offending Indians, known to the citizens of San Juan only as Sanup's Boy and Joe Bishop's Boy, were taken to Blanding for trial. The Indian "boys" were very uncomfortable there, not fully understanding the proceedings and mistrusting the white man's justice. So, the first chance they got, they ran away. It happened during a noon lunch break when the sheriff was momentarily distracted. What really got the local authorities outraged was the fact that the fugitives had outside help in getting away. Someone had horses waiting for them in the bushes.

It was suspected, but never proven, that Old Posey, a local Paiute chieftain, had assisted in the escape. Posey was about sixty years old at the time and an important leader of the non-reservation Indians still living in southeast Utah. A Paiute himself, Posey was married to a Ute woman, and that gave him considerable influence with both tribes. The old chief had a long and contentious history with the good citizens of San Juan County. He was known as a troublemaker and had been arrested for playing a role in the infamous "Indian uprising" of 1915.

The sheriff went in hot pursuit of the jail-breakers, but came back a short time later, empty-handed. The Indians were armed. Shots had been fired and the lawman needed some help. The sheriff promptly deputized "a large number" of well-armed civilian volunteers who formed a posse to hunt the rascals down.

But instead of going directly after the armed and fleeing "hostiles," the posse went to the nearby peaceful Indian village on Westwater Creek and rounded up about "forty squaws, papooses, and a number of bucks" who were taken to Blanding and held in a guarded "compound" or "stockade" that was actually an open cattle pen. It was late March and the weather was cold and snowy.

Some of the peaceful Indians escaped the Westwater roundup and fled south toward Navajo Mountain on the Arizona border. But most were captured a few days later after a running gunfight when two of them were wounded. The fugitives were taken in cattle trucks to join their relatives in the stock corral in Blanding. A few who got away were able to link up with the fleeing jail-breakers and help with the Indian defense.

Newspapers had a field day. Headlines screamed that Indians were on the warpath and southeast Utah was immersed in bloodshed and violence. Civic-minded citizens from all over the territory were quick to come to the defense of home and hearth. New posse members were signing up daily. Armed with modern hunting rifles, dozens of adventurous young men joined the hunt for "wild Indians" while their womenfolk waited at home with tears and trepidation.

The government did not sit idle while her citizens were in danger. Utah's governor wired San Juan authorities offering a state-sponsored airplane, complete with machine-guns and bombs, to aid in quelling the "Indian uprising." General Custer could only have dreamed of such timely and overwhelming reinforcement. The full weight of twentieth century technology, combined with nineteenth century bigotry, was being brought to bear against the natives. Those "murderous redskins" never had a chance.

Old Posey, the aging "war chief," took charge of the Indian retreat and fought a very good rear-guard defense against the aggressive actions of the posse. At least two lawmen had their horses shot out from under them, and a Model-T Ford was peppered with bullets, one flattening a tire and another "passing lengthwise through the back seat on which three sheriff's deputies were sitting." Amazingly, none of the posse members was injured.

But the Indians were hopelessly outnumbered and outgunned. After a long chase across the desert, Old Posey and Sanup's Boy, one of the young men who made the jail break, were both shot from long range with modern rifles. The body of Sanup's Boy was recovered quickly, but Old Posey got away, badly wounded. A U.S. Marshal found his body about a month later.

Old Posey died hard, holed up like a wounded old lion in a secluded patch of junipers on the desert: bleeding, starving, cold, and alone. A fugitive in the land of his fathers, he died without medical assistance or hope for the future, the last of the Native Americans to die in battle in defense of an ancient way of life. Surely, a great assemblage of honored warriors was there to greet him as he walked the star path in the sky to join his ancestors in the land of forever.

Back in Blanding, the Indians held in the stockade, who were guilty of nothing but being Indians, had their children taken away to be sent to an Indian boarding school in Arizona. They were also forbidden to return to their homes and gardens in Westwater Canyon. Instead, each family was given a small plot of land in Allen Canyon, a little farther removed from the white settlements. There, they could starve in peace and quiet solitude.

So ended the last of the Indian wars.

<hr>

The year 1923 was also a time of major consequence for the Allred, Tibbetts, and Moore families. It was the year Winny Allred was arrested for murder.

Wilford Wesley Allred had a good reputation in Moab and Grand County. He had never been in any trouble. Even the newspaper reporter who wrote the initial story of the murder couldn't believe the man was capable of murder. He described Allred as "a peaceable citizen." But he did say that Allred was known to be drinking heavily the past few months, and during a recent trip to Moab, "he did not seem himself."

Winny Allred and his wife Amy had recently divorced after eighteen years of marriage and six children. The divorce weighed heavily on Winny. The man became so distraught that he gave up his music, sold his musical instruments, bought a small herd of cows, and moved to the family homestead in Brown's Hole, trying to make amends. But Amy was not receptive to his change of heart. When he showed up at Brown's Hole, she took the kids and moved to Moab. Winny stayed at the ranch and took up drinking.

The murder happened in January at the ranch in Brown's Hole. Winny was entertaining friends with moonshine and a hot game of poker. Initially, there were four drunks in the poker game, but soon after midnight, only Winny and a farmer named J.V. Ellis remained in the cabin, still drinking and playing cards.

According to Winny's confession to the county sheriff a few days later, he and Ellis got into a drunken argument and the bigger man knocked Winny to the floor and beat him severely. The sheriff recorded that Winny's body showed physical evidence of the beating. Then Ellis began to destroy things in the cabin and throw cast-iron stove lids and fire irons at Winny. In an effort to defend himself, the smaller man grabbed a 30-30 rifle and shot Ellis in the upper chest. The bullet seemed to have no effect on the enraged drunk, so Winny shot him again, this time in the face.

Winny was alone with the body for about twelve hours, until the following afternoon when his brother Hulbert stopped by to visit. Hulbert found Winny deep in despair, sitting near the body of his former friend and neighbor. Hulbert went for the sheriff and Winny was arrested and taken to jail in Monticello. The newspaper said Winny was, "nearly insane with remorse, and has not been able to get any sleep since being placed in the jail."

San Juan County had a tough time deciding whether to charge the man with first or second-degree murder. He was initially charged with second-degree, and might have been released on a $5,000 bond, but before he could raise the money, the charge was changed to first-degree. Winny had to stay in jail without the possibility of posting bail. A trial date was set for late April.

The county had a casual attitude toward prisoners in 1923. Winny could not be paroled, but early that spring he was allowed to go with county deputies and other prisoners to cut cedar posts in the canyons near Monticello. Prisoner work crews were expected to help pay the costs of running the jail. The sheriff made Winny promise that he would not try to escape. Allred was known to be a man who kept his word, so that was the end of the matter.

Unfortunately, Winny was sent to camp early one afternoon to fix supper for the work crew, and while in camp alone, he found a .22 rifle belonging to a sheriff's deputy. He shot himself in the forehead, killing himself instantly.

In Moab, the newspaper came to Winny's defense after his suicide:

"Having known Allred over a long period of time, we cannot conceive of his taking the life of another without having some justification for the act. Quite literally, he was so crazed from drink that he acted on blind impulse or in sudden anger; the true story will now, of course, never be known. Yet Allred's friends—and he had many friends—will never consider him a murderer...

"...These things we do know; that Allred lived an honest, peaceful life; that he was big-hearted, generous to a fault; that he had a high regard for his word, and met his obligations scrupulously. In the face of a record like this, can we, by a mere snap of the finger, brand him as a low criminal and ignore his many estimable traits of character?"

After his mother's divorce and Winny Allred's suicide, Bill Tibbetts tried even harder to take care of his mother and help with his younger half-brothers and sisters.

———·•·———

It was late September 1923, and Bill, Tom Perkins, and Uncle Ephraim were camped in a large rock shelter along the Big Water Wash in Elaterite Basin. They were sitting around an evening campfire, deeply engaged in a council of war.

"Between us, we've got over a thousand head," Eph said, staring blankly into the fire. "Considerin' the dry range conditions and all, I think we ought to sell about half of the herd, at least. With what's left, we can take a hundred or so up on the White Rim and scatter the rest real thin along the river bottoms. If we can get half of the cows through the winter, we'll still have a purdy good bunch to start with again next spring."

"Well, I've been with you now for a little over four years," Bill proclaimed, cradling a cup of coffee in his hands. "But near half of this outfit belongs to me and my mother. And since old Winny Allred shot himself last springtime, these cows are about all she's got between her and the poorhouse. This is the second time the woman has been up against this. We cut her back by fifty percent and that'll cut her income, and my income, purdy considerable."

"Yeah, but we can always save the money and buy new stock when the grass comes back."

"It doesn't always work out that way, Eph. You know that. Besides, these cows are ours. They're home grown and they know this desert country. Hell, we got our own breed started here with that mix of your Mexican longhorn stuff and Mother's Herefords. It'll take us another four or five years to get back to where we are right now if we sell half of them."

"So, what do you suggest?" Eph asked quietly, trying hard not to sound annoyed by Bill's hardheadedness. "The grass here in Laterite is all burned up by drought. And them sheep outfits will be droppin' down off the Big Ledge any day now to winter in here, too. There just ain't no feed, Bill. Sell 'em or watch 'em die. That's how I see it."

"No, by Gawd. I won't do it."

"It's your only choice."

"No, Eph, we've got another choice. And I've been thinkin' long and hard about it, too. Let's take this outfit to the best rangeland there is. Let's move the whole show up on the Big Flat beyond Island in the Sky. You said yourself there's still grass up there."

"Oh, good Lord, Bill. You'd have to fight every rancher this side of the Book Cliffs if you moved up on there. That range is old and well established. Some of the biggest outfits in this part of the country are up on the Big Flat. They wouldn't just step aside and let us in there. No way."

"It's public domain, Eph. Those guys can't keep us out if we decide to go there. They don't own that grass any more than me and you."

"Damn it, Bill. They've got a first-right to that range. It wouldn't be proper."

"Yea, but it would still be legal. I don't know about you, but legal, moral, and proper get all mixed up when my cows are starvin'."

"Naw, I don't like it," Eph said. And then he stood up and turned his backside to the fire, staring out into the stars and the deep desert night. The faint hooting of an owl filtered in through the cedar trees. One of the horses grazing nearby blew through his nose in disgust.

"You remember that story from the Bible that Grandpa Moore used to read to me when I was a kid? The one about King David and the shewbread in the temple? He read it to me several times because he thought it was so funny when I asked Grandma to make me some shoe bread in one of my shoes. Well, anyway, did you ever listen to what really happened in that story, Eph?"

Eph was still standing with his back to the fire, looking out at the stars. He didn't answer or act like he was listening to what Bill was saying.

Bill continued without waiting for a reply. Turning toward Tom Perkins, he began: "As I recall, old King David was runnin' from some bad guys and he was hungry. So were his merry men. They stopped by at the temple for something to eat and the priest there didn't have any grub. All he had was shewbread, that holy stuff they kept there in the temple for doin' the sacraments and stuff. Well, David said it was an emergency, and so he took the shewbread and gave it to his troops to eat. David ate it, too. And in the end, the priest said it was okay since it was an emergency and all. Do you remember that story, Eph?"

"Yeah, I remember it," Eph said quietly, still looking out into the darkness.

"Well, the way I see it, you and me are like King David now. Our cows are hungry like David's troops. We gotta find 'em some groceries. I know it's against the Code of the West to move in on those rich guys up on the Big Flat country, but it's an emergency. It's like eatin' shewbread, Eph. It might have been immoral to do it last year when things were good, but we're in starvin' times now and everything has changed. We gotta go where the grass is. If we don't, we're gonna lose it all. We've worked too hard to give it up and just sell out. I vote we take the whole herd up on top to the Big Flat. I promise to smile and be real polite and try to get along with the neighbors. What do ya say?"

"I'll have to sleep on it," Eph said flatly. He then turned and walked toward his bedroll.

CHAPTER 10

THE FIGHT FOR GREENER PASTURES

A COLD WIND WAS BLOWING FROM OUT OF the west, scattering sand over the crests of the dunes before slamming against the ledges along the Green River channel. The winter sky hung low and overcast, nearly touching the tops of the mesas, but there was no promise of snow in the cold, iron clouds. The men tucked their chins into the collars of their coats and squinted with eyes tight against the blowing sand.

The herd was strung out for more than a mile. The cows kept stalling and bunching up as they scrambled up the steep, rocky trail toward the top of the ridge. From a distance, they looked like a long, thin ribbon of red and brown cowhide wiggling slowly up the mountainside. As the top of the ribbon neared the rimrocks, almost 2,000 feet above the river, the tail end of the herd was still stuck in the willows along the river bottom. It was a tough job to get the cattle to line out and follow each other up the trail. Cows were bawling for lost calves, while the half-grown calves played hide and seek with the cowboys in the willows and rocks. The boys whistled and prodded, crowded and pushed, slapping with coiled ropes and long willow whips, even setting the dogs on a few especially deserving, lazy old bovines.

It took all day to get the herd over the top of the rim and onto the flat country on top of the mesa. It was better country up there, with wide, rolling, grass-covered hills. Much different from the confining canyons, ledges, and greasewood bottoms along the river. It was colder on top, too. The elevation was higher and there were fewer sheltering ledges to cut the wind. But there was grass there, sure enough.

———— ⋅•⋅ ————

On the third day on top of the mesa, they saw the riders coming. They were expecting the visit and wondered why it had taken so long. Cold weather, maybe. Most people with brains were holed up in a cabin somewhere with a good fire and a hot cup of coffee.

OPPOSITE: *Island in the Sky, moving cows*

The three horsemen sat on top of a ridge and watched them for a long time. Eph figured they were trying to count the herd, getting a feel for how many new cows were on the range. Finally, the riders turned down the hill and came riding toward the camp. They were wearing long canvas slickers with the tails spread out behind their saddles, greasy felt hats pulled low over their eyes, and leather chaps flapping in the wind. The riders all wore thick wool gloves, and one had a large red bandana tied over the top of his hat and down over his ears. They rode right up to Bill, Ephraim, and Tom Perkins like they owned the place. No one was smiling and the tension was like far-off thunder before a big storm.

"We heard you was up here," the older man of the three said coldly, staring at Ephraim with eyes like a coiled snake.

"Howdy, Albert," Ephraim nodded. And then, turning to the other two, Eph nodded in polite recognition at each man in turn as he said, "John, Owen."

The other men looked back but showed no signs of recognition or friendship.

Bill recognized John Jackson, the father of the Jackson boys who had bullied him when he was a kid. And he knew the man with the bandana around his ears was Owen Riordan, of the Snyder-Riordan cattle outfit. The older man doing the talking was new to him, and he didn't like the man's attitude.

"This here range is already taken," the big cowboy growled, directing his remark toward Uncle Ephraim.

"It sure is taken, all right," Bill interrupted as he stepped forward. "And we're takin' this corner of it."

The man's head jerked toward Bill with his chin up and his eyes flashing fire. "Like hell, you will. By Gawd, we been here since the nineties and there ain't room for the likes of you and your outfit."

"You better tuck it in and make room then," Bill answered, meeting the man's burning gaze with cool gray eyes that showed neither fear nor intimidation. "We're here to stay and you better get used to it."

"By Gawd, we'll see about that," the man barked, his face flushing crimson and his horse starting to fidget, sensing high emotion from the rider.

"Let's go, Albert," John Jackson said forcefully. "This ain't goin' nowhere but a big fight. We've seen what we come to see. We can deal with this later."

The big man sat up tall in the saddle of the dancing, fidgeting horse. He looked Bill squarely in the eye, and said, louder than he needed to say it, "You'll be sorry you ever came here, young man. I'm too old a cat to be screwed by a kitten." With that, the three riders turned their mounts and hurried off toward the top of the ridge, going back the way they had come.

"Feisty bastard," Bill chuckled.

"Don't misjudge the man," Ephraim warned. "Old Albert Beach is tough as nails and more hardheaded than a granite boulder. And he's a full-fledged deputy sheriff, too. He's wearin' a badge under that coat. He'll have the law and the county court on his side if there's ever any trouble. You better watch your back-trail, Bill. You made him mad and he'll take you down a peg, if he can."

"John Jackson is no one to mess with, either," Ephraim continued. "The man loves to fight and he's accustomed to winning. You shoulda' just buttoned yer lip and let me do the talking. I've known those men for a long time and I might have been able to smooth things over some."

"I'm not afraid of those guys," Bill promised with youthful self-confidence.

"Well, you should be," Ephraim said impatiently, showing a touch of irritation at the younger man's cavalier attitude. "Don't expect any of those men to come at you head-on. They'll get you when you least expect it and when you're not looking. There's more than one way to skin a cat, Bill, and they're not going to fist fight with you. We better all be damn careful up here. There's at least six cow outfits using this range and we've only met three of them so far. The Murphys, Taylors, and Pattersons will probably stop by for a visit in the next day or so. This could get ugly before spring."

"And another thing," Eph said, almost as an afterthought, "Albert Beach works for Heber Murphy, the county sheriff. Murphy's family runs cows up here, too. Don't ever forget it. You don't want to get crossways with the law on this range, Bill. There's a whole lot of family entanglements."

———•◦•———

The Moore, Tibbetts, and Allred cattle operation squeezed their stock onto the range and sprinkled them lightly across the Big Flat, Grays Pasture, Spring Canyon, and Arths Pasture. In spite of the winter weather, the boys stayed with the cows, camping out while keeping a vigilant watch. They went to town in shifts for supplies and a few days off. It was a tough way to run a cow business, but very effective. Losses were few and the men knew at all times the numbers, location, and status of their herd.

The other stockmen in the area were sullen and angry, but they had no legal recourse. The grass was on public domain and grazing was unregulated. The borders of a man's rangeland were determined by his grit and the force of his will.

In such an environment, Bill Tibbetts and Ephraim Moore prospered. Eph had been reluctant to move in on the big outfits at first. The man had a deep-rooted sense of right and wrong. He was not one to give offense to any man, and it took time for Bill to convince him that they were doing the right thing by saving the herd. Sure, the other ranchers might not like it, but it wasn't right for them to hoard the best grass while other stockmen like Bill and Eph starved out. The Good Book said God made rain to fall on the wicked as well as the righteous, and the same was surely true about grass. A few big outfits shouldn't be able to hog the God-given cattle food for their stock alone.

Once Ephraim had made up his mind, the tough ex-marine was a hard man to dissuade. The other ranchers knew him well, and they knew he was not one to trifle with. He might have been a religious man, but like Moses in the wilderness, he was not above smiting his enemies from time to time. In spite of hard feelings, his old cowboy friends were civil when they met him, at least to his face.

But the old cowmen held a grudge against young Bill Tibbetts. They saw him as brash, outspoken, and overly self-confident for a pup who hadn't paid his dues yet. Bill was too quick to argue and too willing to fight, for the likes of some of them, and they didn't like it. Young men were supposed to know their place around their elders. Bill's reputation as the kid who went to reform school for stealing horses followed him everywhere, too. The deck was stacked against the swashbuckling young cowboy. Some of the old-timers were plotting ways to take him down a notch.

Nothing happened right away. The ranchers simmered and brooded, but they took no deliberate action. After a few months of unexpected calm, Bill and Ephraim let their guard down and went about their business.

That spring, Bill began taking his younger half-brother, Kenny Allred, with him to the cattle ranges. Kenny was just nine years old, and Bill felt real compassion for him after the boy's father committed suicide. Bill understood the pain of the loss, and he became the boy's surrogate father, the way Bill's uncles had been for him. Kenny helped with the cows all he could, and Bill began paying him with calves.

On Kenny's first trip with Bill, he rode the first day on a man's saddle without being able to reach the stirrups. Kenny didn't complain, but Bill felt sorry for him, so that night around the campfire, Bill made him stirrups out of some old cinch straps. The improvised stirrups were lined with sheep hide to make them fit and feel better. The new stirrups worked great and they sure made the life of a young cowboy more enjoyable.

It was that same spring, in 1924, when Bill and Kenny found the lower Horsethief Spring. They were moving cows along the Horsethief Trail on top of the mesa, and when it began to get dark they camped for the night in the mouth of a nondescript little canyon near some sand dunes. There were willows and a few cottonwoods there, but no water. On a hunch, Bill got a shovel and began digging in the sand in the bottom of the wash. Cold, clear water came bubbling to the surface. Later, Bill and Ephraim put some water troughs there and it became an important watering place for their stock.

Another time, when Bill and Kenny camped at the Horsethief Spring, they were low on food. Near the camp, Bill found tracks of a porcupine and told young Kenny to track it down and kill it for supper while he (Bill) rode over the ridge to check on some cows. When Bill returned, Kenny had skinned the porcupine and had it hanging in a tree. As they prepared a fire to cook their evening meal, Bill finally shook his head and said, "Damn it, Kenny, I just can't do it. That thing looks too much like a little baby hanging there." Bill and Kenny finished the last of the biscuits that evening while the dog had porcupine for supper.

While running cows on the Big Flat, Bill and Ephraim discovered a herd of wild horses in the Grays Pasture area of Island in the Sky. In the early days, Grays Pasture was a famous place for wild horses. In fact, Grays Pasture was named for a wild stallion that frequented the area in the early 1900s. The gray stallion was such an impressive horse that some of the early ranchers released brood mares there in the hopes of getting a colt from the wild, gray stallion.

In 1924, the king of the wild horses was a white stallion, probably a son or a grandson of the famous gray horse the pasture was named for. Bill and Ephraim watched the herd closely for a time, learning their habits, watering holes, and trails to and from their feeding and bedding areas. They wanted to catch a few of the horses to break to use in their cattle business. Catching wild horses was cheaper than buying domestic stock, and wild mustangs made excellent cowponies for use in the rough country. There were some good young horses with the white stallion's herd, and if he could be caught, the white stallion himself would be a prize to make any cowboy proud.

After some planning, the boys decided to make a wild horse trap on the narrow neck of land that separates Island in the Sky from the Big Flat country to the north. The "neck" was a great place to trap wild horses with only a small amount of work required to build fences.

Wild horse traps were usually made by dragging brush and dead cedar trees into a large "V" that squeezed the horses into a tight corral or box canyon where they couldn't escape. The cowboys would then herd the horses into the trap, rope the ones they wanted and turn the others loose. Wild horses were an asset on the cattle ranges and it was good to let some go free. The mustangs would break trails through the snow in wintertime that the cows could follow, and they would keep water holes open in freezing weather by stomping holes in the ice where they and the cows could drink.

Setting up this particular trap, Bill and Ephraim made a solid, dead tree fence across the narrowest part of the neck. They used the sheer drop of the ledges as a barrier on two of the other sides. The horses would be chased out on the thin, narrow neck where the dead tree barrier would stop them and the cowboys could seal the back-trail by dragging in another dead tree or two to prevent the horses from going back the way they came in. The horses would be trapped and the cowboys could take their pick at their leisure. It was a good setup.

On the appointed day, with the dead tree barrier in place, the cowboys crowded the wild horses and got them moving toward the narrow neck. The unsuspecting white stallion led the herd right into the trap. Bill and Eph dragged the cedar tree gate shut and the horses were at their mercy.

The horses ran from barrier to barrier, trying to find a way out. But the fences were solid and there was no way they could escape. The frightened animals went to the edge of the ledges on the east and west sides and looked over, but then bolted back from the abyss as the cowboys expected they would. Finally, when the herd had quieted down some, the boys got down their long ropes and began moving slowly toward the horses.

The white stallion stood in front of the herd as the men approached, doing his best to protect his mares and colts. Then, desperate and wild-eyed, he whirled to the east and jumped from the ledge. His long white mane and tail splayed out in the wind as the big horse went over the rim and disappeared into the nothingness of the canyon far below. The other horses ran in panicked circles for a time, but none chose to follow their master into eternity.

Bill Tibbetts was sick at heart. The death of that beautiful white horse touched him to the very core. He didn't say anything to the others. He simply coiled up his rope, went back to the cedar tree barrier and moved it away so the horses could escape. Then he rode away without looking back. Ephraim and Kenny both followed, no one speaking for a long time.

For several years after that, the bleached and broken bones of that magnificent white horse could be seen near the Shafer Trail, hundreds of feet below where that old wild horse had jumped. Bill didn't like to ride the Shafer Trail after that. Those old bones always made him sad.

———— • • ————

The rain came back in the summer of 1924, and, for a while, everything went fine for the Moore, Tibbetts, and Allred cattle operation.

CHAPTER II

FRONTIER JUSTICE

WITH THE COMING OF SPRING, EPHRAIM Moore began moving his cows off the high country and back to his established and "rightful" range along the White Rim and Elaterite Basin. The winter grass had saved the herd, and Eph felt it was his duty now to pull back and leave the Big Flat to the previous users.

Bill was reluctant to move back to the slim pickings of the river bottoms. He wanted to stay on the Big Flat. Ephraim didn't argue, he just gathered his own stock and pointed them back down the trail. Bill did send most of his mother's cows with Ephraim, but those wearing his own brand, the T-4, he kept on top of the mesa. It was open range and no one could legally make him move. Besides, he was never one to duck a good fight. He wanted to see what Albert Beach and John Jackson were made of after all the threats they had made last fall. Every time he crossed paths with those men they were sullen and angry. They were even angrier when they learned that Bill would be staying on the Big Flat after Ephraim had moved his cows off.

Running cattle on the open range with few rules and regulations made competition fierce among the early stockmen. With few clear boundaries and not many fences, it is not surprising that thievery was a big problem. Rustling was a quick and easy way to increase the size of a herd and the rewards were great if a person never got caught. Small, unbranded calves were stolen often, and many cowboys kept "running irons" in their saddlebags. The branding tool was used to "fix" or modify a "hard to read" brand on a cow of "questionable" ownership. There were many stories of lonesome cowboys coming onto a cattle range pushing a small group of skinny old cows, and then marketing a couple of hundred steers in just three or four years.

To some cowboys, it was like a game to see who could get away with eating a neighbor's beef. Initially, young Bill Tibbetts was not above playing the game. He rustled up some camp meat in the early days and got into trouble with Uncle Ephraim. When Ephraim discovered what

Bill had done, he was so angry that he took his camp outfit and moved a few miles away, refusing to eat or even be near the stolen beef. Bill was careful after that, not to do anything illegal that might upset the older man. They were partners and they needed to be friends.

In June 1924, Bill killed and butchered one of his own calves for camp meat. Not long after that, another cattleman, A.T. Taylor, came by his abandoned camp and found the entrails, head, and hide. Taylor knew the camp belonged to Bill, and he suspected the calf might have been stolen, or so he said. He rode back to Moab and reported the incident to other ranchers who ran cattle in the area.

Three other ranchers, Albert Beach, John Jackson, and Owen Riordan, the same three who had confronted Bill and Ephraim when they first moved their cows to the Big Flat, rode out to investigate. As a deputy sheriff for Grand County, Albert Beach gave the investigation an official status.

The men rummaged through the abandoned camp and inspected the remains of the butchered calf. It wasn't reported in the newspaper, and it never came out in court, but many years later, a man named Otho Murphy, who was an uncle to the sheriff, and whose family owned the Murphy Cattle Company, told Bill's son Ray that he was there with the ranchers during the investigation. Otho said the earmark on the dead calf clearly belonged to Amy Allred, Bill's mother, but one of the ranchers beat the ear off with a rock to destroy that evidence.

After "investigating" the calf kill, the three ranchers followed "suspicious tracks" down the Horsethief Trail to the Green River where they found ten head of their own cattle in the willows along the river. They said it was obvious that the cows had been driven there, and another cow and calf had been killed during the steep descent by falling off a ledge, making twelve head in all. None of those men ranged cows along the river bottoms and they were sure the cattle had been stolen, even though no brands had been altered and the cows were not corralled. Not far from where they found the cows, they came upon a camp occupied by Bill Tibbetts and Tom Perkins.

The ranchers had a heated discussion with Bill and Tom, there along the river, with each side giving a different account of what happened and what was said. Deputy Beach and John Jackson got their version printed in the newspaper. After the confrontation, the ranchers rode back to Moab to file a complaint with the county court.

Feeling secure in their innocence, and not fully understanding the trouble they were in, Bill and Tom shrugged off the incident and went about their business. They had cattle to care for.

A few days later, Bill, Tom, and little Kenny Allred were camped in Taylor Canyon, working a big herd of cows. Ephraim was in Elaterite Basin, looking after his interests there. It was still morning when Sheriff Murphy and a posse of half-a-dozen men came riding into the camp.

"Hello, Sheriff Murphy, what brings you out here in the snakes and lizards on a fine day like this?"

"I got a warrant for your arrest," the lawman said, very matter of fact.

"A warrant for my arrest? What the hell are you talkin' about?" Bill said with genuine surprise.

"I got a warrant for your arrest on charges of grand larceny, Bill. Stealin' cows. You and Perkins both. I gotta take you back to Moab to face the charges."

"Bullshit," Bill said, rather forcefully. "We didn't steal any cows."

"You can tell it to the judge," the sheriff answered, sitting back in the saddle with his hand on his thigh, right close to the big hog-leg of a revolver he wore on his belt. "My job is not to argue the case. I'm just here to take you in."

"We didn't steal any damn cows!" Tom Perkins interjected from the sidelines, stepping forward in a righteous rage.

"I'm sure you'll get a chance to present your case," the sheriff said curtly, turning slightly in the saddle to face Perkins. A few of the posse members began to fidget and feel for their sidearms.

"Hold on a minute," Bill said anxiously, trying to calm things down a bit. "You better explain this. Whose cows did we steal, and when?"

"There was a complaint filed that you killed one of Albert Beach's calves last week," the sheriff said without emotion. "And you boys drove another dozen head off the range and killed two of 'em in the ledges."

"That's bullshit," Bill growled. "I killed one of my own calves last week, and I can prove it. Those other cows came down the trail on their own. They've been down on the river for a couple a weeks now. We told old man Beach and John Jackson all about it when they came to our camp the other day."

"Did you know whose cows they were?"

"Yeah, I can read a brand."

"Why didn't you push them back up on top, and who killed that cow and calf?"

"Two of them cows died in the quicksand tryin' to get a drink in the river," Bill explained. "I can show you the spot. And we didn't push the rest of 'em back up on top because it was none of our business. Jackson and Beach can take care of their own damn cows, we got plenty to do."

"Well, my deputy and John Jackson tell a much different story," the sheriff said impatiently. "I'm sorry, fellers, but I'll have to take you back to face the charges."

"Damn it, sheriff," Bill said with controlled anger as he reaching out to hold Tom Perkins back. "You and me have known each other for a long time. Hell, I worked for your dad when I was a kid. I'm not afraid to face these charges, but damn it, we can't go with you today. You can see we've got this big bunch of cattle gathered and we haven't even started branding yet. It'll take two weeks to round this bunch up again if we turn 'em out today. We've got to get this branding done and who knows when we'll be back. Tom and me will come in Thursday and turn ourselves in. How's that?"

Before the sheriff could answer, a big posse member stepped down from his horse and walked a few steps toward Bill, swaggering like the big dog in the neighborhood while rolling up his sleeves.

"You don't seem to understand," the man said. "We got a warrant for your arrest and we're takin' you in. You come and go peaceful, or by Gawd, we'll fight."

Bill stepped forward with his fists and his hackles up. "By Gawd, we will," he said, melting the bigger man with his steady gaze and rock solid boxing stance.

The bully stood in surprised silence for a moment, and then peeked back over his shoulder to look for reinforcements. The other posse members were still sitting on their horses, looking on like uninvolved spectators. The sheriff was smiling.

"Get back on your horse, Jake," the sheriff spat. "We don't need none of that."

The sheriff turned back to Bill. "Will you give me your word that you'll come in on Thursday and give yourself up?"

"You got my word," Bill promised.

"And make it Thursday morning so I don't have to spend the day worryin' about it?" the sheriff added.

"Thursday morning. You got my word," Bill promised again.

"And you'll have Tom Perkins with you?"

"Tom and me will be in together," Bill said. And then he gave Tom a quick look with a raised eyebrow. Tom nodded agreement. "You got my word."

"Okay," the sheriff conceded. "I'll be in my office Thursday morning so we can take care of the paperwork."

"Wait a minute," the humiliated bully growled from his seat back on top of his horse. "You're not gonna let this guy just go back to his business. We rode all the way out here to take him in. You can't just let him go."

"I've known Bill for a long time," the sheriff answered. "His word is good enough for me. I'll place him under arrest on Thursday."

With that, the sheriff turned and started riding away. The posse members followed obediently, stringing out in single file, none of them bothering to look back.

Bill, Tom, and Kenny Allred stood for a while watching them go. Then Bill turned to Kenny and said: "Don't just stand there with your mouth open, Kid. Get a fire goin'. We got calves to brand."

JULY 10, 1924

THE TIMES INDEPENDENT

TWO YOUNG MEN CHARGED WITH THEFT OF COWS

William Tibbetts and Tom Perkins were today arrested on a warrant issued from the county attorney's office which charges them with the larceny of thirteen head of cattle belonging to Snyder & Riordan, John Jackson and Albert Beach They will be arraigned this afternoon in the court of Justice C. L. Christensen, and the date for their preliminary hearing will be fixed.

Tibbetts and Perkins are accused of having driven the thirteen head of cattle, most of them yearlings, down a precipitous rim onto the banks of Green River and that two head of the cattle were killed in the descent. The defendants are charged with having attempted to bury the hide and carcasses of the two dead cattle. They are also accused of having butchered a yearling belonging to John Jackson, and of burning the hide.

The owners of the cattle, it is said, followed the tracks of the missing bunch and located the cattle on the banks of the Green River. The owners recovered possession of the ten head still alive.

It is said that other evidence implicating Tibbetts and Perkins has been secured, and will be divulged at the preliminary hearing.

The boys worked hard, and by Wednesday evening they had all of the branding done. They rode all night to reach Moab by Thursday morning. Kenny slept most of the way sitting in the saddle while Bill led his horse. By mid-morning on Thursday, Kenny was at his mother's house in Moab, and Bill and Tom were in jail.

———— • • • ————

Once in jail, Bill and Tom Perkins secured the services of Knox Patterson, the only available lawyer in town. Unfortunately, the man was a member of another cattle ranching family in the Big Flat area. Moab was a small town in an ocean of wilderness. There was a small gene pool and almost everyone was related.

The lawyer wanted a retainer to secure his services, but Bill and Tom didn't have any money. Finally, they negotiated an agreement in which Bill signed over his brand. It was a fairly common practice. By signing over the brand, the lawyer secured a lien on anything wearing that brand, be it cattle, horses, saddles, tack, or whatever else, until the legal fee was satisfied. It was a good deal for the lawyer.

A few days later the ambitious young attorney was in court defending Bill and Tom at a preliminary hearing. The newspaper printed a summary of the hearing (following page).

———— • • • ————

After the preliminary hearing, Bill and Tom were taken back to their jail cell. There was no way the boys could hope to make bail. Two thousand dollars each was impossibly steep and Bill was mad at their attorney for not arguing for a lower bail. He was also angry that he and Tom had not been allowed to speak in their own defense. Later that evening, their attorney came to the jail to consult with his clients.

"That was a damn poor performance in court today," Bill growled angrily. "I sure as hell expected better from you. Why didn't you stick up for us when you had the chance? You just sat on your hands and let those lying buzzards and their lawyers walk all over us. Why didn't you argue for a lower bail, for Gawd's sake? This could go on for months. We got work to do, and besides, the chow in here would gag a maggot. You should stop by for breakfast in the morning."

The young attorney in the expensive suit sat in brooding silence for a time, rolling a pencil in his fingers with his face all pinched up tight. He then went off on a tirade of his own.

"There isn't much I can do for a couple of outlaws like you," he said angrily. "You boys are in big trouble. More than you know. They've got a whole trainload of evidence against you they haven't even presented yet, and when they do, you two are likely to hang. I'm not kidding. You might get the death penalty before this thing is done. You ought to pray to God they only give you thirty years. Hell, bitch at me for not doing a good job. Nobody could get you two out of this mess. My advice to you is to bust out of here and run like hell. It might be your only chance."

"I want my brand back," Bill said with angry eyes.

THE TIMES INDEPENDENT

HELD TO ANSWER FOR COW RUSTLING

William Tibbetts and Thomas Perkins Must Face
Serious Charge in District Court in August

William Tibbetts and Thomas Perkins were held to answer to the district court on two charges of grand larceny, by C.L. Christensen, justice of the peace, Tuesday. Their bond was set at $1000 each on each charge, making total bail of $2000 for each of the defendants.

On one charge, Tibbetts and Perkins were accused of butchering a calf be-longing to Albert Beach, this occurred on or about June 17, 1924. The other charge accuses them of stealing and driving away twelve head of cows and calves belonging to Snyder & Riordan, Mrs. Jessie Riordan and John Jackson. The alleged offenses took place on Horse Thief point on the Green River.

The preliminary hearing commenced Tuesday morning before justice Christensen, and continued most of the day. The state was represented by C.A. Robertson, special prosecutor, and County Attorney Charles Kelley, while the defendants were represented by Knox Patterson.

The state assembled five witnesses, and the defense one. A.T. Taylor was the opening witness for the state, and stated that he had ranged cattle in grays pasture and along the Green River for many years. Tibbetts and Perkins, the two defendants, moved onto the range last spring. Tibbetts told Taylor that he was a fast worker, and expected to work so hard the other cattlemen could not stay there. Tibbetts, according to witnesses, suggested that Tibbetts and Taylor work on each other's cattle and see who would last the longest. On June 17, Mr. Taylor and his son Bliss were riding on Horse Thief point, looking after horses and they ran across a recently made fire in which the hide, head feet and entrails of a calf had been buried. A short distance away they saw a number of cattle, and one of them a cow belonging to Albert Beach, showed signs of having recently lost her calf. They saw several horse tracks and followed them, running across Bill Tibbetts. Tibbetts said Perkins was at their camp. Mr. Taylor stated that he reported the incident to Albert Beach and O.V. Riordan upon his arrival in Moab about the first of July.

Bliss Taylor, the state's second witness, corroborated much of the testimony given by his father.

Albert Beach stated that when he was advised of the affair he with Mr. Riordan and John Jackson left for the Horse Thief point country to investigate. They reached the place where the fire had been, and examined the feet and a piece of hide of the animal that had been butchered. Then they took up the trail of a bunch of cows which had been pushed off the Horse Thief point onto Green River. The tracks showed evidence that the cattle had been driven rapidly down the trail, which is very rough and very seldom used. One cow, belonging to John Jackson had fallen over a cliff and was killed, and a similar fate befell a calf belonging to Mrs. Riordan. The three cattlemen, in descending to the Green River bottom where their stock never range, found ten head of cows and calves belonging to Snyder & Riordan and John Jackson. The cattle were badly skinned up and showed rough treatment. They drove the bunch back up on top and then returned to the Green River bottom, where they found Tibbetts. They accused Tibbetts of driving the cattle off, and he denied the charge. He finally offered, however, to make it right for the cattle killed rather than to be arrested. The witness said Tibbetts admitted butchering a calf on Horse Thief point, but insisted it was his own animal. According to the witness, Tibbetts said he burned the hide because it was his own and he could do what he wanted to with it. He said he could prove the calf was his, and said Tom Perkins was with him.

Mr. Riordan was next examined, and his testimony was practically the same as that given by Mr. Beach.

John Jackson, one of the prosecuting witnesses, was called by the defense. He was asked if the charges preferred against the defendants was not a frame up deal to get them out of the country. The witness denied this.

After the arguments of the respective counsel, the justice held the defendants to answer to the district court on both counts, setting the bail at $1000 for each defendant on each charge.

The case will probably be heard at the August term of the district court.

"To hell with you," the attorney hissed. "This trial might go on for months and you don't own enough to make it worth my time. I'll be working for nothing before we see the end of this. I should have made you sign over your pocketknife and belt buckle, too."

With that, the lawyer in the shiny shoes stood up and rattled a tin cup on the bars to summon the deputy. Before he walked out, he turned, smiled sweetly, and said, "We'll try to have a more pleasant discussion sometime next week after you boys have had time to simmer down some. In the meantime, you can hire another attorney if you think it'll do you any good. I think the nearest good one is over in Grand Junction."

As the lawyer and the lawman walked away down the street, the boys could hear the lawyer talking to the deputy: "Those thievin' bastards have some nerve to be criticizing me. Abe Lincoln himself couldn't win an acquittal for those two."

JULY 24, 1924

THE

TIMES INDEPENDENT

COURT WILL CONVENE AT MOAB AUGUST 18

The August term of district court for Grand county will convene at Moab on Monday, August 18. Judge George Christensen will preside. Three criminal cases are on the calendar for trial. They are State of Utah vs. Edward Cottrell, murder in the first degree; State of Utah vs. James Warner, murder in the first degree, and state of Utah vs. William Tibbetts and Thomas Perkins, grand larceny. It is stated to be improbable that all of the criminal cases will be tried at the coming session, and it is possible that a change of venue in the Cottrell case may be asked. This case was tried in May, resulting in a hung jury.

After that, the jail cell got very dark and very small. Bill and Tom stood at the window bars and watched the moon come up over the mountain. There was a whole big world out there and they were stuck in jail. Thirty years? Life? A hangman's noose? Neither of them slept at all that night.

Moab City Jail House 1900s

CHAPTER 12

THE GREAT ESCAPE

LIGHTNING FLASHED ON THE MOUNTAIN and thunder rolled across the valley. Big drops of rain dripped from the roof of the jailhouse and splashed in little puddles in the darkness. A cool breeze filtered in through the window bars on the iron door.

"Is that you, Joe?"

"Yeah."

"What'ya got?"

"Shut up, Bill, we're still makin' sure nobody's around."

Bill's younger brother Joe was standing outside of the jail while his companions snooped around the neighborhood. The Moab jail sat off by itself, a little ways from other buildings, and the jailer went home at night leaving the prisoners there by themselves. There was no streetlight. The outside of the jail was as dark as the inside. It was a good setup for a jailbreak.

Finally, another voice whispered from outside. "Looks good, Joe, there ain't anybody around."

"Is that you, Sog?" Bill asked. Sog Allred was Bill's half-brother, one of Winny Allred's sons.

"Shut up, Bill," was the whispered reply, again from his nervous brother, Joe.

A moment later the end of a heavy metal bar came in through the window bars on the iron door, almost hitting Bill in the face in the dark.

"Good Lord, Joe, What ya doin? I thought you had a hacksaw."

"Pry bar from the county road shed," came the answer. "Stand back."

The pry bar locked against the window bars on the massive iron door as pressure was applied from outside. Metal began to squeak and bend. Grunts, groans, and heavy breathing could be heard out in the night as three or four men pushed, pulled, and strained against the heavy pry bar. Rivets popped and iron plate bent.

Finally the pry bar was jerked back outside and a face appeared in the open space between the bent and twisted bars. "Can you get out through that?"

"I'm not sure," Bill offered.

"Let me try, I can do it," Tom Perkins insisted. He was real anxious to get out of jail. The prisoners slid a chair over to the door and Tom climbed up on the chair and started out through the bent bars on the window, head first. He squeezed, puffed and panted, but quickly became stuck, halfway in and halfway out.

"I'm stuck, boys. I can't make it."

"Be quiet, damn it. Don't make no noise," came the whispered reply.

Three sets of hands took hold of Tom anywhere they could get a grip. One took the arm sticking through the bars, another got his head and another his shoulder with a grip on his armpit. On cue, all three began to pull for all they were worth.

"Agggg, wait ... don't ...Gawd, you're pullin' my damn head off ... jeez ... I can't breathe." The men turned him loose and he hung there, hopelessly stuck.

From behind, Bill stood on the chair, wrapped his arms around Tom's waist, put one foot against the iron door, and with a mighty heave he pulled Tom back into the jail. Both men crashed to the floor in a tangle of arms, legs, and chair.

"Damn, I think you broke my elbow," Tom groaned, rolling around and gasping for breath on the jailhouse floor. There was a knot on his head and his ribs were bleeding where the metal door had peeled his hide. Bill laughed while untangling himself in the darkness. "For a man who hates jailhouse food, you seem to have gained a few pounds, Tommy, ol' boy."

"Shut up in there, damn it," Joe hissed from the window bars. "You're gonna wake up the whole darn town."

Bill slid the chair back up to the window while Tom nursed his wounds on the floor in the dark. On the chair, Bill stuck both arms and his head through the opening in the bars, and with a little help from his friends on the outside, he was able to squeeze through with only a few scrapes and bruises. Then the boys put the pry bar back against the window bars and, with Bill's help, they were able to open the gap another inch. Tom was able to wiggle free on his second attempt. Bill went back to the window and stuck his head back inside the jail.

"Are you coming with us, Ed?" Edward Cottrell was in the jailhouse, too, waiting to face his second trial for murder in the first degree. His first trial had ended in a hung jury. His second trial, on the same charge, was coming up in just a few weeks.

"No, Bill, I can't go with you."

"What are you thinking, Ed? Here's your big chance to get out of here."

"I'm innocent. I'm going to stay and face the charges."

"Well, I'm innocent, too, but I'm not gonna let 'em hang me for it."

"Tell Joe not to worry. I won't say nothin' about who broke you out," Ed promised. "I'll tell 'em I didn't see nothin'. You can count on that."

"Well, okay, if that's the way you want it. I hope it all works out for you, Ed. Good luck. We gotta go."

In the dark alley behind the jail, Joe gave Bill and Tom their getaway instructions. "There's a boat tied to the big cottonwood down near the old swimmin' hole on the river. In it we got purdy well everything you boys will need to lay low for a few weeks. Keep an eye out for Uncle Ephraim. Once the dust settles, he'll be bringing supplies to the cow camps along the river. He'll be watchin' for ya."

Bill and Tom thanked their partners in crime, but the pry bar crew had no time for small talk.

"You better get movin' and put some river between you and town before it gets light," the nervous Joe admonished. "We gotta get this pry bar back to the county road shed and then we're all goin' home so we can wake up in the morning and be surprised that you broke jail, just like everybody else in town."

"Thank you, brother, you saved our lives. We won't forget this."

"Shut up and head for the river," Joe mumbled as he reached out to take his older brother in an awkward handshake.

Bill shook his brother's hand and then pulled him close, put his arm around his neck, knocked his hat off and messed up his hair, just like he had done a million times when they were kids. "Thanks, Dody," he said, using his kid brother's pet name. "Tell Mother I'll write."

———⋅⊹⋅———

The storm clouds departed as the morning sun touched the canyons of the Colorado. Two men in a boat were drifting along with the current, taking inventory of the supplies they found in the boat. Bill and Tom's saddles were there, along with a wooden box containing flour, beans, bacon, and canned goods. There was also a canvas sack with a small frying pan, a couple of tin cups, a butcher knife, a salt sack, a can of coffee, a canteen, and a tin of matches. There were a few items of clothing lying about the boat like they had been thrown aboard as an afterthought: a couple of shirts, three pairs of old socks, a couple of bent-up straw hats, a small tarp, some rope and a pair of gloves. Wrapped in a scrap of canvas, they found one of Ephraim's old rifles, a Winchester 30-30 with three boxes of bullets. Bill's .44 Special revolver was there, too, with a cartridge belt full of ammunition. Bill had left the gun at his mother's house before turning himself in to the sheriff. The boys decided they were pretty well equipped, considering the circumstances.

The canyons were clean and bright after the summer rain and the air tasted like freshly scrubbed pinyon and rabbit brush. The boys reveled in their freedom. They decided to drift on down to the confluence of the Colorado and Green rivers and stash the boat and supplies there. They would then walk the 15 or 18 miles up the Green River to the mouth of Horse Canyon where they could access the Laterite country on foot. There were horses they could catch there, and they had camp equipment cached at a couple of cow camps along the Green River. They kicked back in the boat and congratulated each other on making such a fine and well-equipped escape.

———⋅⊹⋅———

Confluence of the Green and Colorado River

In the late afternoon they were still drifting along, enjoying the scenery and their newfound freedom, when Tom sat up straight and turned to face back up the river.

"Listen, Bill," he said with some alarm.

"What?" Bill asked.

"Can you hear that hum? There's an echo in the ledges. Sounds like a motor. But there ain't no roads around here anywhere."

"Oh, my God," Bill whispered. "I'll bet it's that damn motorboat from the Moab Garage Company."

"What we gonna do?" Tom's eyes were big and his mouth hung open after the words had fallen out.

"Grab that other oar and paddle like hell. We gotta get off the water. If it's the sheriff and they catch us on the river, we're dead meat."

As the echo in the ledges grew louder and louder, the boys paddled harder and harder. They were motivated and they made the water fly. They beached the boat in some willows, grabbed what few survival items they could gather up in a hurry, and began scrambling up the steep hillside away from the river. They were near the mouth of Standing Rock Canyon, about 15 miles up the Colorado from the confluence with the Green River.

Their fears were well founded. It was the sheriff in the motorboat. After the jailbreak was discovered early that morning, the law officer had trailed the fugitives to the bank of the river, following their tracks in the mud. The sheriff then rented the only motorboat in town, a launch belonging to the Moab Garage Company that was usually used to haul miners and oil workers up and down the river. The boat was small so there were only three posse members aboard: Sheriff Murphy, County Commissioner Mel Stewart, and Deputy Sheriff Albert Beach. A man named Ross Thompson was also there as helmsman and captain of the ship. He was an employee of the company that owned the boat.

Many years after the event, Ross Thompson told Bill's son, Ray, his version of what happened next. Thompson's story is much different from what was reported in the newspaper. His story is more like the one Bill Tibbetts told his sons. In deference to the law officers involved and the sensibilities of their families, Thompson didn't reveal this information until 1984. By then he was the only surviving eyewitness of the incident.

Kenneth Westwood provided a second corroborating account. Ken wrote down what Bill Tibbetts told him about the affair back when the two of them worked together in the 1940s. Westwood's story fits hand in glove with Thompson's account.

———·◆·———

"Over there, in the willows. That's got to be their boat," Deputy Beach called over the roar of the engine while pointing to the north bank of the river.

The engine was throttled back and the boat turned sharply toward the shore. The three law officers picked up their guns and scanned the rims above the river for any sign of the fugitives. The boat operator cut the engine just shy of the riverbank and the boat went skimming in over the waves, stopping with a thump against the wet sand. The boat sat rocking slightly with waves lapping against the sides. The passengers stood up to get out, and that's when a rifle bullet hit the water alongside the boat with a smack like a beaver's tail on the water. The thunder of the rifle shot echoed in the ledges, reverberating like a tuning fork. The lawmen dived onto the sandbar and then piled up on top of each other in the willows, cursing and clawing for cover.

"That shot hit purdy close," Tom Perkins observed from his hiding place on a rocky rim, a few hundred yards above the river and the cowering law officers.

"The closer, the scarier," Bill grinned. "I didn't intend to hurt any of those fellers, but I think I got their attention. What do you think?"

For a long time nothing happened. The lawmen couldn't see out of the willow thicket to locate the fugitives. The fugitives couldn't see the lawmen in the willow thicket. Everyone just held their ground and waited to see what would happen next.

Finally, Tom spoke. "Bill," he whispered, "There's one of them sneakin' off to the right there. He's headed for those big rocks."

"Good deal," Bill whispered back. "Let's let 'em get a little farther away from the boats. We gotta get back down there and get some more of our stuff. It's a long ways up on top of the mesa and we're gonna need some of those things."

"The other three are moving now," Tom said. "They're in those big boulders. See that big flat rock down there by those cottonwoods? They're just to the left of that."

A short time later a tiny head popped up like a prairie dog from behind a big rock, and then another, and another. "They're gettin' kinda brave down there," Tom, the observer, pointed out.

The roar of the 30-30 took Tom by surprise. A puff of dust exploded in the middle of the big flat rock and the ricocheting bullet went screaming off into the atmosphere. The slug hit several yards from where the heads were peeking up, but the heads all disappeared in an instant and never showed themselves again.

"Can they hang a guy twice for breakin' jail and shootin' at the sheriff?" Tom asked with a worried voice.

"Naw, once usually does the trick," Bill said with a wry smile. "What the heck? If they're gonna hang us, we might as well give 'em a good reason. What we got to lose?"

Soon it was dark and the canyon got very quiet. Bill took a chance and sneaked down to their boat to recover more supplies while Tom stayed above and threw rocks once in a while to make noise and keep the posse occupied and on guard. Bill also took a few items from the sheriff's boat and dumped other stuff overboard into the river. He then disabled the sheriff's boat by adding water to the gasoline tank.

When the sun came up the next morning, the sheriff and his posse were still pinned down along the river while Bill and Tom held the high ground with their rifle. The sheriff's party had spent a miserable night hunkered down in the willows while being eaten alive by millions of mosquitoes. Bill and Tom shared a can of peaches as they sat in a cool, bug-free morning breeze, keeping an eye on things down along the river.

Finally, later that morning, Bill called down to the sheriff. "Do you guys want to lie there all day in the hot sun and mosquitoes, or would you rather go home?"

It was an easy decision to make. The sheriff called back that they would leave if Bill promised not to shoot. A truce was negotiated and the sheriff and his men took to the river and started back for Moab.

THE
TIMES INDEPENDENT

ALLEGED COW THIEVES STAGE JAIL BREAK

Make Get-away Down Colorado River in Boat; Sheriff and Posse in pursuit

After prying off two of the bars on the front door of the county jail, William Tibbetts and Thomas Perkins, charged with cattle rustling, made their escape from custody at about one o'clock this morning. The two prisoners, who evidently had outside assistance, broke through the jail door with a heavy crowbar.

Tracks left by the escaping men indicated that they went down the Colorado river in a boat. A posse led by Sheriff Heber Murphy is today in a motor boat in search of the fugitives.

The escape of the two alleged cow rustlers took place, it is thought, about one o'clock. Ed Cottrell, who was being held in the jail awaiting trial for murder, states that he was awakened by the noise made by Tibbetts and Perkins breaking the bars of the jail door. Cottrell states that the men apparently had outside assistance, although he did not see anyone outside the jail. Tibbetts and Perkins forced the bars with a large prybar. They advised Cottrell to remain in bed. After their departure Cottrell looked at his watch and it was twenty minutes after one o'clock, so states Cottrell, who made no attempt to escape from custody, advised the officers about eight o'clock this morning of the jail-break of his fellow prisoners.

Sheriff Heber Murphy's first thought was that the men had gone down the Colorado river in a boat. It being assumed that they would attempt to reach the rough country along the Green river, where they range their cattle, and where they are familiar with all the trails and hide-out places. Several row boats on the river below Moab were checked by the sheriff, and one was found to be missing. A skiff owned by C.A. McLeod, which had been kept on the sloughs below town during the summer, was found to have been dragged to the river, several hundred yards distant. A riding bridle was found lying on the shore where the boat was put into the stream this discovery indicates that Tibbetts and Perkins took along their saddles and outfit, and that they have horses cashed at a convenient point along the river.

As soon as the trail of the escaping men was found, Sheriff Murphy made arrangements to start in pursuit. The gasoline launch of the Moab Garage company was rented, and the sheriff, accompanied by deputy Albert Beach and Commissioner Mel Stewart, with Ross Thompson for pilot and boatman, started down the river at two o'clock today it is figured that the fugitives have about twelve hours the start.

In the event that Tibbetts and Perkins attempt to reach their cattle outfit by boat, which would necessitate going down the Colorado some eighty miles to the confluence with the Green, and then rowing up that river some forty miles, the officers in the power boat may be able to overtake them. However, it is thought likely that the fugitives have horses cashed down the river some twenty or thirty miles below Moab and in this case they will be able to reach the "robbers' roost" country along the Green river before they are overtaken by the sheriff and posse. The country along the Green river, where Tibbetts and Perkins range their cattle, is exceptionally rough, and the fugitives might be able to evade capture there for a long time.

That Tibbetts and Perkins are heavily armed there can be little doubt. The officers who left in pursuit took along a number of rifles and a large supply of ammunition. Six Moab cattle-men are riding the Tibbetts – Perkins range on both sides of the Green river, and all will doubtless be deputized in the hunt for the escaping prisoners They include O.V. Riordan, John Jackson, A.T. Taylor and A.D. Holyoak.

There is a possibility that Tibbetts and Perkins went in some other direction, possibly by automobile, and pushed the row boat into the river and left the bridle on the shore as a blind to put the officers on the wrong trail. As a precaution, officers of neighboring counties have been notified to be on the lookout for them. It is thought certain, however, that the men went down the river to the country they know best, where their chances for escape would be greater.

That the prisoners had outside assistance is certain, as some-one furnished them with the crowbar, with which they broke through the door. It is also thought likely that their outside confederates got their saddles and a camp outfit ready for them, so that they would lose no time in making their get-away.

In breaking jail, the two alleged rustlers committed a further crime. The person who furnished them with the crowbar committed a felony punishable by imprisonment for a term not exceeding three years, and a fine not exceeding $1000.

Tibbetts and Perkins were being held in jail pending trial in the district court on a charge of grand larceny. They are charged on two counts; one of the offenses being the butchering of a beef belonging to Albert Beach, and the other the theft of thirteen head of cattle belonging to John Jackson and Snyder & Riordan. In default of bonds in the sum of $2000 each, Tibbetts and Perkins were placed in jail to await their trial.

On account of the extreme heat, none of the prisoners in the county jail have been locked in the cells, according to Sheriff Murphy.

The men made their escape with ease, as the bars on the front door are not strong and it is not believed it took them ten minutes to pry off a couple. No attempt has been made to keep people away from the jail, and it was doubtless a simple matter for an outside friend to pass a crowbar and possibly other implements through the bars to the prisoners.

This is not the first jail break that has been staged at the local jail, as prisoners have made their get-aways from the institution at least half a dozen times in the past. This is the first instance, however where the bars have been pried off, the usual method being to cut a hole through the roof.

It is freely predicted that serious trouble will be experienced in capturing Tibbetts and Perkins. They are said to be men who would not hesitate to kill if this became necessary to retain their liberty.

From their perch on a rocky rim, Bill and Tom watched as the posse retreated. They were happy to see them go, but it was a bittersweet victory. They had won the first round, but they knew the real fight had just begun. They were in big trouble now. Breaking jail and shooting at duly sworn law officers was no small matter. They knew the sheriff would soon be hot on their trail again and he would be mad as hell for all of the mosquito bites and humiliation.

The posse's version of the encounter, as told in the newspaper, is much different from the story told by Bill, Tom Perkins, and the riverboat man, Ross Thompson.

AUGUST 7, 1924

THE TIMES INDEPENDENT

OUTLAWS ELUDE OFFICERS WHEN OVERTAKEN DOWN COLORADO RIVER

Bill Tibbetts and Tom Perkins Make Escape to Rimrocks;
Are Now in Rough Country Between the Rivers

Bill Tibbetts and Tom Perkins, accused cow rustlers who escaped from the Grand county jail last Thursday morning are still at liberty, having succeeded so far in evading the officers searching for them. They are now thought to be in the rough country between the Colorado and Green rivers, where, it is conceded, they may be able to evade capture indefinitely.

Tibbetts and Perkins, who escaped down the Colorado river in a row boat, were overtaken Friday afternoon by Sheriff Heber Murphy and posse, who went down the river in pursuit of the fugitives in a motor boat. The officers, rounding a bend in the river some six miles above the junction of the Colorado and Green rivers, came upon the fugitives boat, which they had evidently quitted in great haste only a few minutes before. Apparently Tibbetts and Perkins had heard the motor boat while still several miles distant, and had decided to make a break for the rocks. Their boat was left with its nose in a sand bar, and the tracks of the two men indicated that they were in a great hurry in getting away. They left their entire outfit in the boat, taking with them a supply of food. The sheriff and his posse, consisting of Deputy Albert Beach, Commissioner

Mel Stewart and Ross Thompson, stopped their motor boat on the sand bar and the sheriff started to look over the contents of the smaller boat. As he was doing this, the fugi-tives, who were apparently hiding in the rocks above, fired a shot, apparently for the purpose of throwing a scare into the officers. Sheriff Murphy and Deputy Beach then took up the trail of Tibbetts and Perkins, while Commissioner Stewart and boatman Thompson stayed with the boat to prevent the cow rustlers from getting possession of it.

The sheriff and his deputy trailed the fugitives for about ten miles. The tracks led back up the river several miles, and then headed up the north rim in a northerly direction towards the Green river.

Apparently the fugitives had given up all intentions of returning to their boat, as their trail led in a direct route towards their cattle range along the Green river, which was no doubt their objective. It was useless to attempt to follow them, as the country is probably the roughest and most inaccessible in the west. After following the men for eight or ten miles, the two sheriffs returned to the river, and it was decided to give up the chase for the time being. Accordingly the officers started back to Moab, a day and a half being consumed in the return trip. They reached Moab Monday night. Tibbetts and Perkins had evidently intended to go in their boat to their range along the Green river, some forty miles above its junction with the Colorado. However, they had no oars, and for this reason made rather slow progress down the river. They took with them in the boat their complete camp outfit, including saddles, a bed, their boots and spurs, and a supply of food. All of this was left in the boat when they ran to the rocks. Among the articles found by the officers in the boat were the outfit mentioned, together with two boxes of cartridges, a sack of flour, baking powder, coffee and preserves. Tibbetts and Perkins no doubt gathered up some provisions before their hasty departure from the boat, as particles of bacon wrapper were found on their trail. They probably have enough supplies to last them a week or more.

The officers left the stolen boat and its contents on the sand bar where it was beached by the fugitives. It would have been impossible to have towed the boat back to Moab. The trail of the fugitives headed directly towards their cattle range and indicated that they had no intentions of returning to the boat, and the officers saw no reason for destroying the boat and its contents.

Sheriff Murphy and Deputy Beach left Moab Tuesday on horseback for the country where it is thought Tibbetts and Perkins are in hiding. The officers will deputize a number of cattlemen now in that section and a vigorous hunt for the fugitives will be conducted. The plan will be to guard the trails and the few water holes, as it is believed the men will show up sooner or later. However, it is recognized that Tibbetts and Perkins may be able to evade capture indefinitely, as they know that country like a book and are well versed in the art of roughing it in the hills.

It is thought possible that the fugitives are short of ammunition, as two boxes of .30-.30 cartridges were found in their boat. The officers believe they overlooked the cartridges in their hasty departure, although they may have an additional supply with them.

Although Tibbetts and Perkins were not seen by the officers down the river, there is little doubt that the sheriff and posse were on the right trail. While it is possible that the river excursion could have been pulled off by friends or the fugitives in order to lead the officers on a blind chase, this theory is not seriously subscribed to. The natural place where Tibbetts and Perkins would seek to evade capture is the rough country along the Green river, where they are so familiar with the surroundings and would be at a decided advantage in outwitting their pursuers.

No word has been received from Sheriff Murphy and Deputy Beach since they left on their second trip for the outlaws. Among the people who are assisting them are Special Deputies Felix Murphy and Dale Shafer. A.T. Taylor, O.V. Riordan, Otho Murphy and several other cattlemen are also along the Green river and will no doubt cooperate with the officers in trailing the fugitives.

The Island in the Sky mesa, as seen from Junction Butte in Canyonlands National Park

CHAPTER 13

FUGITIVES ON THE DESERT

AFTER WATCHING THE SHERIFF AND HIS posse start back up the river with the boat engine spitting, coughing, and belching smoke, Bill and Tom went down to their boat and retrieved the remainder of their supplies and equipment. They then carried everything, in two or three trips, away from the river and cached nearly all of it in a small, sheltered alcove among the rocks. They kept only the bare essentials to take with them, intending to come back on horses to retrieve the stash. With sage limbs they erased their tracks to the cache as best they could, counting on the desert wind and a promised summer rainstorm to finish the job. It was almost dark when they finally topped the White Rim and began walking north to find the Shafer Trail. They walked along the edge of the rim on the slickrock to avoid leaving any tracks. Luck was with them and their path was lit by moonlight as they made their escape from the river.

Bill and Tom won their footrace to the top of the Shafer Trail and the Big Flat. It took the sheriff and his posse most of three days and nights to travel the 45 miles back to Moab and sound the alarm. In spite of what was reported in the newspaper, the sheriff didn't spend that time looking for outlaws, he was slogging along on foot in the brush and mosquitoes of the river bottom, trying to get back home. The sabotaged boat motor had quit him just a few miles upstream from where he left the outlaws.

The sheriff's delay in getting back to town gave Bill and Tom time to climb the Shafer Trail, catch some of their own horses on the Big Flat, retrieve their cached goods, and disappear before the second posse arrived on the scene.

Back in Moab, Sheriff Murphy deputized the ranchers who were Bill and Tom's accusers and set them on the trail like a pack of bloodhounds. Those men knew the high country, the Big Flat and Island in the Sky, and they knew the two fugitives. But no one knew the White Rim and the river bottoms like Bill and Tom. The outlaws would be damn hard to catch down under the rims.

Back in town, Bill and Tom's families were questioned at length. Someone had helped the boys escape and the sheriff wanted to know who did it. Ed Cottrell, the man who refused to escape with Bill and Tom, was true to his word and never told the sheriff what he knew. Years later, he would tell Bill's son, Ray, all about the night his father broke out of jail.

By Wednesday, six days after the jailbreak, Sheriff Murphy and his posse were camped in the Big Flat while scouring the countryside for the fugitives. What they didn't know was that Bill and Tom had watched them make camp, and after dark that first night the boys had crawled up so close they could hear the men talking. The sheriff and posse members were sitting around a campfire drinking coffee and discussing plans for running the outlaws down. The fugitives were hiding in the bushes nearby and listening to every word. It was an entertaining evening for the two young outlaws and it provided them with valuable information. Later that night, the boys discussed running off the posse's horses, but decided not to do that. The posse might get discouraged and go home if they couldn't find the fugitives. The boys decided to watch and wait rather than provoke the lawmen.

For a week or two, Bill and Tom kept hidden in the roughest parts of the rugged country. They traveled on slickrock at every opportunity to keep from making any tracks; and when they moved, they took extra horses. Extra horses were good insurance if a fast getaway was needed, and extra horse tracks confused the lawmen. Posse members were looking for the boot tracks of two men or the tracks of two horses. When they cut a trail made by four or five horses, they naturally assumed it was made by another group of posse members out doing their civic duty.

——•·•——

But it didn't take long for the outlaws' supplies to run low. The getaway boat had been stocked with enough food to last for a couple of weeks, and a couple of weeks went by fast. On one occasion, driven by hunger and a mischievous spirit of sweet revenge, the boys were able to sneak into the posse camp during the day and steal items of food and supplies while the lawmen were out beating the bushes to find them. But it was risky business and they were almost caught. The lawmen kept an armed guard at their camp after that.

Finally, when the pressure got to be too much, the boys abandoned the high mesa and dropped down to the White Rim above the river. They had a secret hideout there in a big cave just under the rim. Bill had found the cave a few years earlier while setting traps. The cave could be accessed on slickrock without leaving any tracks and it was big enough to accommodate horses. An added bonus was a spring of cold, clear water at the back of the cave. The outlaws spent several days in that hideout.

——•·•——

"Well, that's the last of the food," Tom said as he tossed an empty tin can on the trash pile at the back of the cave. "What now?"

"We got a lot less stuff to pack," Bill replied.

"Yeah, but we're getting' purdy sucked-up, too. We're gonna have to get some groceries somehow, and purdy soon. You got any suggestions?"

"I wish I'd a showed this place to Uncle Eph," Bill said. "I'll bet he's out looking for us by now. And he'll have panniers full of grub. He'll stash stuff at our old cow camps if he can't find us."

"Yeah, but we can't get to any of our old cow camps. That posse is out for blood. I've never seen citizens so dedicated. They've got every trail and river crossing covered and they ain't lettin' up. We're trapped here under this rim."

"Aw, they'll get tired one of these days and go home," Bill insisted.

"They've already done that and come back again with fresh horses." Tom complained. "And it seems like more posse members show up with each new group. You musta really put a burr under that sheriff's blanket when you nailed him to that sandbar with that 30-30."

"Yeah, he might have taken it personal," Bill smiled. "I'll bet the voters are all laughing at him, too. He'll want to take us home tied over his saddle like a couple a dead deer, just to get even."

"Do you think they might really shoot us if they catch us?"

"Damn right. That no-good lawyer said we might hang for cattle rustlin'. Add a jailbreak and shootin' at the sheriff to that, and we've committed a capital offense. They'll shoot us down like a couple of mad dogs. It'll save the expense and trouble of going to trial."

"Well, one thing's for sure," Tom said. "We'll have to get us a new lawyer if they do catch us and take us back alive. That last one didn't work out so good."

"You don't know the half of it," Bill said with a wicked grin. "I'll bet that lawyer is madder than the sheriff."

"Why's that?"

"Well, you know that attorney kept badgering us to pay him up front. But I didn't want to pay the guy until he earned his fee. Heaven knows I got nothin' against paying a day's wages for a day's work, but when he kept insisting that he wasn't going to help us unless we paid him first, I got suspicious. So, when he suggested that I sign over my brand, I thought it was a good idea. He's now the proud owner of the Rocking-T."

"But your brand is the T-4," Tom said, somewhat perplexed.

"That's the one I use, all right," Bill smiled. "But I own the Rocking-T, too. At least I did until I signed it over to that lawyer guy. I started using the Rocking-T back when I first got out of the army. I haven't used it for years."

"Oh, my Gawd," Tom said with his eyes wide and his hand over his mouth. "You mean you signed over a brand with no property attached to it?"

"There might be a crippled-up, three-titted old cow out there someplace still wearin' that mark," Bill laughed.

"We're in bigger trouble than I thought," Tom moaned. "No wonder that sheriff and posse are so damned hot on our trail. That slick city lawyer is beatin' the drum and kickin' everybody out of town to go hunt you down. You made a damn fool out of him, too."

"I'd a made it right with the guy if he'd done us a good job," Bill insisted. "But I was suspicious right from the start, especially since his relatives run one of those cow outfits trying to kick us off the range. Lookin' back on how it all turned out, I think I did the right thing. What do you think?"

"You'll be the death of us yet, Bill. Is there anybody in Grand County you haven't got mad at us?"

"The women all love me," Bill smiled, posing dramatically with a hand inside his shirt like Napoleon. "There's somethin' about handsome outlaws that attracts women like flypaper."

"Well, I hope women are attracted to skinny outlaws, cause that's how we're gettin' to be. I've taken my belt up two notches already. What we gonna do about getting somethin' to eat?"

"We got lots of bullets but we can't shoot," Bill reminded him. "Those lawmen will come like vultures if they hear us shoot. So, getting' a deer or shootin' a beef is out of the question."

"If we could rig up some fishing line we might get some catfish out of the river," Tom said hopefully. "But we ain't got no hooks."

"We can dig more sego bulbs and set a few more rabbit snares," Bill suggested. "Fat rabbit goes down pretty good when you can catch one."

"Yeah, but we've been catchin' more chipmunks than rabbits," Tom complained. "Now, don't get me wrong, I'm not above eating another chipmunk. It's just that when we divide up a chipmunk, I think I ought to get the hams once in a while instead of just the shoulders."

"You crybaby," Bill laughed. "I caught that chipmunk all by myself and I deserved to get the hams. You catch your own chipmunk if you want a bigger share."

"Chipmunks must be the bottom of the barrel for us outlaws," Tom said wistfully, "I never figured on any of this when we were planning that jailbreak."

"It can still get worse," Bill assured him. "Those Paiutes used to eat lizards, snakes, and grasshoppers to survive out here in this country."

"Would you really eat a snake?" Tom asked.

"Damn right," Bill promised. "I'll eat grasshoppers, too, before I'll go back to that jailhouse. I'll eat my horse, saddle, boots, and belt before I'll walk out of here and surrender to that sheriff."

The boys sat for a while contemplating the seriousness of their situation. Then Bill looked over at Tom with deep and brooding eyes. His mood was suddenly deadly serious. "No, by Gawd," he said. "I'll be like that white stallion over on the narrows. I'll jump from one of these damn ledges before I'll let that sheriff put me in chains. Nobody is gonna hang Bill Tibbetts."

After a pause, Tom said quietly, "I'm with you on that, Bill. I'll jump, too."

Neither of them spoke for a long time after that. They were thinking.

———•—•———

The boys never got around to eating their saddles and boots, but they starved down enough to eat a few grasshoppers. In fact, Bill and Tom lived on grasshoppers for most of a week.

The Paiutes roasted crickets on the hot coals of a fire. Bill and Tom tried grasshoppers cooked that way, and they weren't bad. Of course, they weren't good either. Next they tried the big bugs boiled in water, sun-dried, and dipped in salt. But they still tasted like grasshoppers, no matter how they fixed them. So finally, they just picked them off the bushes and ate them raw and cold, picking their teeth with the long, wiry legs.

Bill joked that it didn't take long to get all of the grasshoppers he ever wanted to eat, but eating grasshoppers did give him an advantage. After a few days of eating grasshoppers, he could outrun any rabbit on the desert and catch it with his bare hands. It might be that eating grasshoppers makes a person run real fast, or, maybe he just wanted to catch that rabbit real bad. Either way, a fat rabbit was in big trouble when grasshopper-eatin' Bill Tibbetts was around.

———•·•———

Late one morning during the starving times, the boys were on horseback in Holeman Basin on the White Rim above the Green River. They were desperate and looking for a calf they could rope and kill with a knife for food. But as they topped a rise they spotted several horsemen off in the distance toward the north, coming their way at a fast clip. It was the posse. They had been spotted and the wolf pack was on their trail.

The boys turned and fled toward the south, staying on the White Rim. A few miles down the rim they passed under Grand View Point and continued following the White Rim on the Colorado River side toward Moab. They were purposely leaving a good trail that was easy to follow. But once they were well ahead of the posse and out of sight around the point of the mesa, they turned their horses to the slickrock edge of the White Rim and doubled back the way they had come. Before the posse came in sight they had dropped down a secret trail under the White Rim and hid in their outlaw cave. A short time later they could hear the posse riding past only a short distance above them on the rim. The boys held their horses' noses to keep them from whinnying and hoped the posse wouldn't spot the scuffmarks on the slickrock where they had traveled. They could hear men talking and the clatter of horseshoes on the rocks as the posse passed overhead and continued on their way.

Just when they figured the posse had passed them by, they heard the clicking of hooves coming around the slickrock shelf to their hideout. The men looked at each other with wide and frightened eyes. They were trapped. The jig was up. Surrender or fight? Kill or be killed? Both men raised their guns, not knowing what to expect.

The sound of hooves got louder and louder until a big fat desert bighorn sheep walked around the corner and then froze like a statue, there in the sunshine. The big ram rolled his eyes in surprise at the men and horses standing in the shadows only a few feet away. The men stared back over the sights of their guns. The sheep licked his lip in nervous anxiety and then turned stiffly and walked away, going back the way he had come, acting as if he knew the outlaws had been there the whole time.

"Good Gawd," Tom gasped, relieved to the point of giddiness. "I thought we was goners for sure."

"I'll bet he was comin' to this cave for a drink of water," Bill said. "Did you see how fat that old buck sheep was? I'm so hungry I almost shot him, to hell with the sheriff and the posse. We gotta get outta here and go somewhere we can shoot some food, Tom. We're starvin' to death. I'm ready to let the sparrow hawks have the grasshoppers. Let's get out of here where we can shoot a deer, or a beef, or a rabbit. Anything. Hell, I can smell those roasted sheep chops and that old sheep took them with him."

"That posse is still purdy darn close, Bill. I'm afraid they'll spot us if we make a run for it."

"Damn them to hell," Bill growled. "They'll spot us anyway if we stay here. In just a short time now they'll be figurin' out we gave them the slip and they'll be comin' back along this rim lookin' for where we went. We're trapped in this cave like a couple a rabbits in a cage. The only chance we got is to go off this rim where they can't follow."

"There's no trail off this rim," Tom said with some alarm.

"That's why they won't follow us," Bill said with his mind made up. "If we go back on top and try to outrun them, the only way we can go is north, up the Green River where they saw us this morning. If we do that, they'll chase us all the way to Vernal. All the trails and river crossings are covered by lawmen, you know that. We probably won't make it, especially when they start using those doggone telephones and automobiles."

Bill continued, "But if we drop off this rim to the river, where there isn't any trail, we'll probably kill our horses and ourselves getting down, so they won't follow, even if they see our dust. They're not that desperate. And once we get to the river – if we get to the river – we got several choices as to which way we can go and they won't know which choice we made. It'll give us a good head start to make our getaway."

"I knew you'd get us killed one of these days," Tom grumbled as he stuffed the 30-30 into his saddle scabbard.

"Shut up and tighten your saddle cinch," Bill warned. "We might as well go for broke. No sense stayin' here and riskin' a gunfight. I'm tired of eatin' grasshoppers and I'm ready to make a change. If we die, we die. It's time to follow that old white stallion to hell."

It really was a suicide mission, an act of complete desperation. The horses were aimed at the rough country near the confluence of the Green and Colorado rivers, that impossibly rugged landscape below Grand View Point. The outlaws and their horses went straight down from the White Rim into red sandstone and steep talus slopes toward the river bottoms. The Green River was more than a mile away and more than a thousand feet lower in elevation.

The descent was unbelievably steep and treacherous. And once they were committed, the boys had no possibility of ever turning back. The horses slid down the near-vertical slopes in the shale, sand, and gravel. Sometimes the horses skidded down on stiff legs and sometimes they slid on their backsides, nostrils flared and eyes wide with terror. The cowboys clung to the horses desperately, sometimes in the saddle and sometimes sliding in the dirt alongside the animals. Showers of loose rocks tumbled down the steep grade ahead of the struggling animals, bouncing and skipping over the ledges and crashing into the canyon below. They scrambled over rocks, brush, and cactus, through deep ravines and off low canyon walls, jumping when there was no other way to get down or around an obstacle.

Finally, somehow, they broke out on the riverbank near the cool and welcoming waters of the Green River. The horses were skinned and bleeding, the men scraped and bruised, the saddles scuffed and covered with dirt, but they had made it, alive and still with the horses. Their gamble had paid off. If the posse ever figured out where they went, no one bothered to follow. Bill Tibbetts was right about that. The lawmen were not that desperate.

JULY 28, 1924

THE
TIMES INDEPENDENT

OFFER REWARD FOR CAPTURE
OF TIBBETTS AND PERKINS

The board of county commissioners held a special meeting Friday, with Commissioners Stewart and Hammond present. Sheriff Heber Murphy was authorized to offer $100 in cash for the capture of William Tibbetts and Thomas Perkins, wanted for cattle stealing, who recently escaped from the Grand county jail. A reward of $50 will be paid for the arrest of each man.

AUGUST 14, 1924

THE
TIMES INDEPENDENT

MAN-HUNT CONTINUES WITHOUT SUCCESS

Sheriff Murphy Again Leaves On Trip Down Colorado River In Quest of Jail-Breakers

After Searching for six days in the rough country between the Colorado and Green rivers in an unsuccessful attempt to locate Bill Tibbetts and Tom Perkins, cow rustlers who escaped from the Grand county jail, Sheriff Heber Murphy, Deputy Albert Beach and Special Deputies Felix G Murphy and Otho Murphy returned to Moab Sunday night. They spent nearly a week in the country where it was thought the outlaws were hiding, but failed to find any trace of them. The officers found Tibbetts's and Perkin's saddle horses, but there was no sign that the fugitives had returned to their cattle range for horses. The sheriff and party hunted most of the time on foot, as the country is too rough for horse travel. They carefully cut sign all through that territory but could not find a single clue that indicated the men had returned to their old habitat along the Green River.

Sheriff Murphy and Deputy Beach went on foot down towards the Colorado river, where Tibbetts and Perkins had escaped, to the rimrocks after leaving their boat when overtaken by the officers two weeks ago. No tracks were found to indicate that the men had continued towards the Green river, and hence it is assumed that they went back to their boat on the Colorado river. It is the opinion of the officers that they returned to their boat and are now attempting to get out of the country by river.

Sheriff Murphy left yesterday morning on another trip down the river in a motor boat, piloted by Ross Thompson of the Moab Garage company. He will ascertain definitively whether or not the outlaws went back to their boat. If they continued in the boat, the sheriff may follow them in an attempt to head them off. It is possible that they have continued on down the Colorado and up the Green in the boat, and may yet show up on their cattle range.

Failing in this attempt to capture the men, Sheriff Murphy will return to Moab and again leave by horse and pack outfit for the desert, in a second attempt to track them down.

THE
TIMES INDEPENDENT

FUGITIVES THOUGHT TO BE OUT OF STATE

William Tibbetts and Thomas Perkins, who escaped from the county jail at Moab three weeks ago, are now well out of the country, in the opinion of officers who have unsuccessfully searched for them following their escape. Sheriff Heber Murphy who, with O O Morgason and Ross Thompson, made a second motor boat trip down the Colorado river last week in an effort to determine where the fugitives have gone, returned Monday. They found that the boat and supplies left by Tibbetts and Perkins when they were overtaken by the first sheriff's party several days after the jail break, had not been molested, and the supplies were intact. This proves that the outlaws did not return to the boat but had continued on foot towards the Green river. No doubt they secured horses there and are now out of the state.

Sheriff Murphy and party had a strenuous time negotiating the river with their motor boat, last week due to the extremely low water and the many mud bars deposited by floods, their boat was in the sand the major portion of the trip, and they were compelled to wade and pull their craft. The trip required six days.

It was reported in Moab this week that Tibbetts and Perkins had been seen at Castle Dale, and were on their way to Nevada. This report is unverified and its authenticity is doubted. The officers of all surrounding counties have been notified of the men's escape and it is possible the fugitives will be picked up. Sheriff Murphy has not given up the chase and states that he is confident the men will be apprehended.

CHAPTER 14

A LETTER TO THE EDITOR

AFTER ESCAPING FROM THE POSSE, BILL and Tom crossed the Green River and made their way into Elaterite Basin. Bill and Ephraim kept food and supplies stashed there in a shallow cave along the Big Water Wash. The boys were almost starved when they got to the place, and, to their delight, they found that Ephraim had recently stocked the wilderness pantry, knowing that the fugitives might try to get there. The boys made a feast of beans, rice, and cornmeal. They were also able to shoot a deer without fear of alerting the posse, and a diet of buckskin and biscuits soon had them in top form.

Elaterite was farther out on the desert than the Big Flat area where most of the posse members were searching for the two young outlaws, but Bill and Tom knew it was risky to stay there for long. They figured the posse had probably found the skid marks in the shale where they dove off the rim, and the sheriff might suspect Elaterite Basin would be their destination, if they survived.

But the outlaws had an ace in the hand they were playing. Neither the sheriff nor any of the posse members knew the trails in and out of Elaterite, and that gave Bill and Tom a big advantage. The boys camped for a few days and rested, watching their back-trail closely, knowing the way out if a posse did show up on the horizon.

While they were there, Uncle Ephraim stopped by to visit. He just happened to be in the area checking on his cows.

———•+•———

"Well, I'll be damned, ain't you two a sorry sight. I heard you got killed gettin' away from old Albert Beach and his posse. They said you idiots went right off the White Rim and probably died there under the ledges along the river someplace. I expected your bones would wash up down by Hite or Hall's Crossing one of these days."

"Good to see you, Eph. You saved our lives with that big box of grub. How's Mother, and how are things in town?"

Elaterite Basin, in the Maze

"Amy sends her best," Eph smiled. "But she's sure been worried about you two. Old Sheriff Murphy camped out in her kitchen for quite some time trying to sweet talk her into telling him who broke you outlaws out of jail. She finally had to tell him to get the hell out of her house. Feisty woman, that mother of yours."

"Wish I could have seen it."

"Joe and Sog and the rest of the boys are all doin' real fine. Everybody's healthy, happy, and goin' about their business. Last I heard the only prisoner in the Moab jail was some drunk from Grand Junction."

"That's good to hear. What happened to Ed Cottrell?"

"Ed got a change of venue. They sent him to Price so he could get an impartial jury. He changed his plea from innocent to involuntary manslaughter and they sentenced him to 18 months in the state pen. The judge allowed time off for what he already served in the county jail, so they figure he'll be back home in about six months."

"I hope things work out for him," Bill said. "Me and Tom sure tried to get him to come with us. Ed's a purdy decent guy. Keeps his mouth shut, too."

"And how are you getting' along, Eph?" Bill continued. "Have you caught any grief over any of this?"

"Oh, I had a visit from the sheriff and old Albert Beach, too," Eph smiled. "They didn't ask me any questions, just warned me that helpin' you outlaws in any way was against the law. They said they're gonna keep a close eye on me until you boys are back in jail where you belong."

"What did you tell them?"

"I told 'em to get the hell outta my house, too."

Everyone laughed.

"But I do have a problem," Eph said. "There's still a hell of a lot of work to be done with these cows, and me and little Kenny are havin' a tough time keepin' up.

We've got steers to gather and a trail drive to make to get these beeves to the railroad."

"We'll help you all we can," Bill promised. "You keep the line camps supplied with groceries and we'll bunch all of the steers we can find. We should be able to help here in Laterite and along the river bottoms, but we won't be able to go back over on the Big Flat. Too many concerned citizens. You'll have to gather my stock over there. "

"I'm sure we can help each other out," Eph said. "But before you boys do too much with the cows, I think you should lay low for another week or two. I expect Sheriff Murphy to be here in Laterite in the next few days. That posse figured out that you monkeys went over the rim, and when they don't find your bones along the river, they'll probably come lookin' for you over here. If it was me, I'd take the North Trail outta here and go hide out on the Roost for a while. I'll stay here for a few days to cover your tracks and have a polite little get-together with the posse when they show up."

"Sounds good," Bill agreed.

"You fellers take one of the packhorses and all the grub you can carry. I brought a couple a wool blankets and some other things you might need. And I got a stack of old newspapers for you to read, too. You boys have been purdy famous since your big jailbreak. I though you might want to read all about it. I'll bet you didn't know you got a bounty on your ears like a couple a sheep-eatin' coyotes."

Bill and Tom took Ephraim's advice and rode out of Elaterite Basin along the North Trail and into the Robbers Roost. There, they vanished amid the canyons and sand dunes of Butch Cassidy's old hideout.

The boys found a shallow cave that fit the requirements for an outlaw hideaway, and they settled in to spend the winter.

"Well, I guess this is home," Tom said with just a touch of melancholy as he cleared a flat spot at the back of the cave for his bedroll. "I always liked campin' out, but I never figured that one day I'd be hidin' out like a wild Indian."

"This is a great spot," Bill assured him. "We got everything we need. We got grass and water for the horses. We got shelter from the wind and snow. We got firewood and deer tracks in the cedars. We got two or three good escape routes with plenty of places to cache supplies. And we can see the whole country from here. What else would an outlaw need?"

"Oh, I don't know. There's this girl named Wanda who lives over by Monticello who said if I ever get lonesome I should…"

"Oh, knock it off," Bill growled with an amused smile. "We got no room for Wandas in this outlaw camp. You wanna see Wanda you better go surrender to the San Juan county sheriff. Maybe they'll lock you up in the jailhouse in Monticello and Wanda can stop by for a visit."

"I'll bet she'd bring me a cake with a file in it," Tom grinned.

"Come here and take a look at this," Bill said, changing the subject. While they had been talking, he had been carving his name into the sandstone wall of the cave.

Tom walked over and read the inscription. It said:

My Home
Bill Tibbetts
Sept. 15, 1924

"What do ya think?" Bill asked. "You want to put your name there, too?"

"Looks like something they might put on your tombstone," Tom said with a wry smile. "I think I'll pass."

"Well, if you ain't the most depressing soul to talk to. I think it looks purdy. Kinda homey like a welcome mat."

"People wipe their shitty feet on welcome mats."

"That's why I put it near the ceiling, asshole."

———————

Once safely settled in their outlaw camp, the young men were incredulous when they read about their exploits in the Moab newspaper. The story in the paper wasn't anything like the real-life adventure they had experienced. To their dismay, the sheriff and the posse had reported the facts all wrong. They laughed when they read about how Sheriff Murphy and Deputy Beach had chased them for ten miles up Standing Rock Canyon. The way they remembered it, the good sheriff and his right hand man were pinned down in a mosquito-infested swamp the whole time. There was nothing about the sabotaged boat motor and the sheriff walking all the way back to Moab, either.

The boys found the newspaper stories amusing, but the half-truths and outright lies really got their dander up. They were frustrated because there was nothing a couple of self-respecting outlaws could do to set the record straight. Until finally, after stewing about it for a few days, they decided to fight fire with fire. With righteous indignation and in the spirit of fair play, they wrote a long letter to the editor of the Moab newspaper, explaining their point of view on the whole matter. They were pleasantly surprised when the letter was actually printed, with a few omissions, of course.

It is interesting to note that the letter is dated September 16, just one day after Bill carved the inscription in the outlaw cave. It took another month for the letter to find its way to the offices of The Times-Independent newspaper in Moab.

⁘

"Oh, Bill, is it really you?" his mother said as she reached out to hug her wayward son. "We've been so worried. All those men leavin' town with guns to hunt for you and Tom. I've been worried sick.

"Aw, me and Tom can take care of ourselves," Bill grinned. "Let's pull down the window shades so no one can see I'm here."

"Where's Tom?"

"He stayed at our camp over on the Roost. We got horses to care for and somebody needed to stay with our stuff. I just came to town to get us some winter clothes, boots, and a couple more blankets before it snows out there on the desert."

"How in the world did you get to town without the sheriff catchin' you?"

"I worked it out with Sog. We been sendin' notes through Uncle Ephraim. Sog picked me up just out of Green River in old man Tomlinson's Ford truck. We drove here right down the main road. Until it got dark, I just ducked whenever we passed another outfit. Sog's gonna take me back in the morning with a load of potatoes."

"You had better be careful, Bill."

"Sometimes the best place to hide is right out in the open," Bill smiled. "People don't look for you there."

"Let me fix you something to eat. I'll bet you haven't had a proper meal for weeks."

"That'd be great Mom. By the way, I got a letter here I want you to take to the post office in the morning. It's to the editor of the newspaper. They've been tellin' lies about me and Tom. I've got to set 'em straight on some things

OCTOBER 16, 1924

THE TIMES INDEPENDENT

⸻

THE PAPER RECEIVES A LETTER

Bill Tibbetts and Tom Perkins, Escaped Jail-breakers, Take Their Pen in Hand to Tell Us All About It

From their hide-out on "Wildcat Bend" in the rimrocks and inaccessible canyons along the Green river, Bill Tibbetts and Tom Perkins, alleged cow thieves who escaped from the county jail on the night of July 30 by breaking through the bars of the front door, have written The Times Independent an extended letter in which they give "their side of the case"

The letter was received by The Times Independent Tuesday morning. The envelope was postmarked October 14. Inclosed with the letter giving the fugitives version of the cow stealing case, was a brief note to the editor, signed by J W. (Bill) Tibbetts, asking that we publish the attached communication. The note follows:

Moab, Utah, Oct 13, 1924
Editor Times-Independent:

Dear Sir. I am sending herewith a letter stating our side of the case that was framed up against Tom Perkins and myself. Would like to have it published, but if you don't feel like giving us a fair hearing return the letter to Amy E Allred.

Respectfully
J.W Tibbetts

The note to the editor was written under the date of October 13, the day before The Times Independent received the letter at the postoffice. The note is also dated at Moab, Utah. Whether the fugitives came to Moab to post the letter, or whether they sent it to the postoffice by a friend, is of course unknown to us.

In the letter which they asked to have published, Tibbitts and Perkins claim that they were the victims of a frame up on the part of other cattle men on whose range they had intruded. They assert, in effect, that there was a general conspiracy on the part of their accusers, the prosecuting office, the county commissioners, the town paper, and in fact half the town to blacken their reputations and give them a rotten deal all around. They state that accounts of their arrest, hearing and escape from jail as published in The Times Independent were badly overdrawn and exaggerated, and offer to give us and exaggerated and offer to give us (sic)

They claim their preliminary hearing was a farce. They have a few uncomplimentary things to say about the judge who heard their case, they pay their respects to the prosecuting attorney, they harshly criticize and condemn their own attorney who represented them at the trial, and finally they severely castigate the sheriff for the treatment accorded them in the county jail.

For two reasons The Times Independent would like to publish verbatim the communication from Tibbitts and Perkins. First, we endeavor at all times to print both sides and versions of any criminal case which comes before our courts, and we try to be just as fair as possible in the presentation of news matter: second, the communication from the fugitives would prove entertaining and perhaps somewhat amusing to a large portion of our readers. However, the authors of the letter have not conformed to proper newspaper style in framing their letter. They make positive assertions which possibly could not be proved in a court of law; the words "perjurers," "liars," "bribe," "thieves" and similar complimentary references appear quite frequently. The co-authors are perhaps unfamiliar with our libel laws, which make a newspaper publisher legally responsible for the matter which appears in his paper. Naturally The Times Independent has no desire to jump into a libel suit, and therefore we are unable to give publicity to the communication in its entirety. We nevertheless wish to oblige the boys to as great an extent as we consistently can do, and we will attempt to fairly print "their side of the case" by deleting certain parts of the epistle which are considered libelous.

In according space to the communication, it is needless to say that The Times Independent does not vouch for any of the statements made therein. We are merely following our usual policy of placing our columns at the disposal of the people for the dissemination of news with absolute fairness to all. Times-Independent readers will recall the evidence in the Tibbetts-Perkins case as published at the time of the hearing. We now are privileged to present to them "the other side of the case." The communication from the fugitives, with certain parts necessarily deleted, follows:

Wildcat Bend, Green River
Sept. 16, 1924
"Times-Independent:

"We have read the accounts published by The Times-Independent of our arrest, hearing and escape from the county jail, and in most cases the facts were badly overdrawn and exaggerated, probably on account of misinformation on the part of the reporter.

"It might have occurred to some of your readers there could be two sides to our case. If The Times is willing to give us a fair hearing we would like to state a few facts concerning our case and the treatment received by us while in the custody of the sheriff.

"In the first place the charges made against us were made upon a little bit of doubtful circumstantial evidence (such as some three-weeks-old horse and cattle tracks, and a cow said to have been seen bawling a half mile from where we had killed a beef) sworn to by a number of cattlemen * * * *. The only thing they had in the way of evidence was their own lies, for example when they swore that one of us (Bill Tibbetts) had offered to pay for the cattle killed on Horsethief point. The main reason for our arrest was the fact that we had put some cattle on a part of the range used by our accusers and they wanted to get rid of us. They have been in the habit in the past of keeping cattle and sheep off this range by threats of violence and where threats didn't work by the wholesale stealing of stock put on the range * * * *. In our case threats had availed them nothing so they tried persecution by getting the county to hold us while they and others jumped onto our backs. The prosecuting bunch, the county commissioners, the town paper, and all of the false accusers in Moab and vicinity united to exaggerate all of the false rumors that have been circulating about us for years, and give us a rotten deal generally. To start with our hearing was a farce * * * *. The prosecuting attorney and others were overheard talking about our case so we knew that it was already fixed that we were to be bound over and our bonds boosted.

"After we were taken through the formality of a hearing we were bound over and placed under two thousand dollar bonds each, which they knew we couldn't give, all * * * * that they might keep us under lock and key while they went about to circulate lies, and create prejudice against us.

"We might have bore the outrages already mentioned but the alleged food served us at the county jail boarding house was simply unendurable. A conglomeration of bread, meat, and vegetable scraps called Scrappo, refuse and offals from tables, donated by neighbors to feed the chickens, was served to us along with dried scraps and crusts of bread, obtained from the same source. Wilted, unstrung string beans, seasoned with scraps of meat of questionable quality left on our plates from previous meals. Such stuff was served us and hunger forced us to eat small quantities of it until we found a cat tooth in the Scrappo (the house cat had disappeared a few days before) when we refused to eat it, but the same mess was served up day after day (apparently it was that or nothing) and onions were added in an effort to kill the odor. Our friends brought us in cake, pie and other edibles which kept us alive and we would have stayed and stood trial in the district court and proved to the citizens of Grand county that our persecutors had but slight cause to even accuse us (Here follows a somewhat caustic criticism by the defendants of their attorney and his handling of the case). That was going one too strong for us so we decided to leave, which we did on the night of the 30th of July.

"We went down the Colorado river and on account of shallow water and sandbars our progress was slow by day, so we camped at night and as a consequence was overtaken by the sheriff's posse in the motor boat. We left our boat about

five minutes before the posse arrived and took to the rough hillside. When the motor boat landed some of the men got out and were looking around on the sand bar for signs of us. We fired one shot into the air and they all took refuge under the river bank. Beach was sitting in the rear end of the motor boat and you'd a thought he had wings to have seen him cross the sandbar. We had previously agreed between ourselves to submit to capture rather than shoot anyone, so when the men went under the bank we laid our guns down by the rock where we sat, and walked away.

"We have been branded as thieves, desperadoes, and murderers, and have had our characters dragged through the mire by people who are anxious to drag our reputations down on a level with their own, fed on slop by the side of which six days eating grasshoppers seemed like a picnic. We were told on one occasion that there wasn't anything very good to eat but it was good enough for dogs.

"We wouldn't mention this food question (for we consider anyone that would take advantage of people because they are in jail to feed them slop that is unfit for a swine to be entirely beneath our contempt) only that the county commissioners might know what kind of treatment the county's prisoners are being subjected to, and what the county's money is being paid for, and perhaps prevent the same thing happening to somebody else. Of course we all understand that everything must be kept in the family.

"We are not trying to pose as examples of innocence, but when we are stoned to death we would like to have someone found among our accusers that is at least as honest as ourselves to throw the first stone. We have heard that the law reads that a man is to be considered innocent until he is proven guilty, but in our case we were considered guilty and treated as convicts right from the start.

"We have no hard feelings even against our accusers for having us arrested or for anything they told that was the truth, it is their lies that we resent.

Tom Perkins
Bill Tibbetts

Robbers Roost Area

CHAPTER 15

THE PHANTOM ON THE MOUNTAIN

FOR THE NEXT SIX MONTHS, BILL AND TOM hid out on the Robbers Roost. From caches near their old cowboy camps they were able to put together a decent camp outfit, and they were able to shoot deer to supplement the supplies Uncle Ephraim left for them at prearranged drop sites. With Ephraim acting as their cowboy courier, they were able to send and receive notes from family and friends and keep up on events in Moab by reading old newspapers. Overall, they fared quite well.

Sheriff Murphy did show up in Elaterite Basin to question Ephraim and look for any signs of the fugitives, but his reception was cool and he found no evidence the outlaws had been there. Things quieted down after that. The weather turned cold and posse members were volunteers who had other things to do. In addition, some people still thought the boys might have been killed in their wild escape to the river. Others suspected they had left the country. Either way, there was no sense in following a cold trail in the middle of the winter. Better to sit by the fire and wait for the fugitives to show up somewhere before resuming the chase.

However, at least one posse did attempt to venture into the Robbers Roost. One day in October, Bill spotted a string of riders coming down the Green River from the north. From a high rim he kept an eye on them as they made camp for the night on the Moab side of the river in Potato Bottom. Early the next morning, Bill and Tom were watching as the lawmen broke camp and prepared to cross the river.

The posse looked like a bunch of younger men, and they were apparently inexperienced. The outlaws watched with some amusement as the lawmen loaded their pack animals and then sucked the packsaddle cinches up as tight as they possibly could. They did the same to their saddle horses. Any old-timer could have told them to loosen the cinches. When a horse swims, he needs to fill his lungs with lots of air to keep afloat.

The fugitives watched as the lawmen dropped down into the cold and turbid waters of the Green River, where they were soon in big trouble. The heavily loaded horses couldn't swim with their cinch straps so tight. The animals fought, floundered, and sank beneath the waves. Saddle-horses, too, thrashed violently and went under. The men struggled, screamed, and swam for their lives. Men were throwing ropes to each other and running up and down the riverbank trying to rescue horses and other men. It was a terrible thing to witness.

From their vantage point in the rimrocks across the river, the morning sun felt warm and welcome as the fugitives watched the lawmen struggling in the cold water, mud, and morning shadows of the river bottom. The far-off squeals of struggling horses and the shouts and curses of panicked men echoed in the ledges and rippled away down the canyons. As far as Bill and Tom could tell, none of the men drowned, but several of the horses were lost to the river.

The outlaws took no delight in watching the tragic scene. They had great respect for good horses and they felt bad for the inexperienced souls who had spurred them into deep water with loads too heavy and cinches too tight. Later that day, they were still watching when the wet, cold, and discouraged lawmen took the back-trail for home. Some posse members were walking and most of their packhorses and supplies were gone. The story of the misadventure was never reported in the newspaper.

———— ·—·—· ————

The fugitives didn't waste time while hiding on the Robbers Roost. They gathered cows. They worked the rims and river bottoms pushing steers into Elaterite Basin where they could be bunched for a cattle drive. Ephraim and young Kenny Allred worked the White Rim while Bill and Tom took care of the deep desert canyons that were a little farther removed from the prying eyes of civic-minded citizens. They were cautious and always watching their back-trail, but there was no sense to sit idle when Ephraim needed some help. What's more, a good many of those steers belonged to Bill's mother.

Unfortunately, most of Bill's stock was still over on the Big Flat country where Albert Beach, John Jackson, and Owen Riordan were still on the prod. He would have to figure out how to gather them later.

By late fall, the cowboys had a herd put together and they started out of Elaterite for the railhead in the town of Green River. They pushed the steers up the North Trail and into the cedar ridges and rolling sand hills of the Robbers Roost. It took a few days to go around Barrier Canyon and bend the line of travel back north toward the Book Cliffs. They crossed the San Rafael River and went straight for the railroad tracks and holding pens at the edge of town.

With the cattle tucked safely in the railroad corrals, Bill and Tom left Green River quickly and rode forty miles to the little town of Hanksville. There were fewer lawmen around Hanksville, and no one ever asked any questions there. In that sleepy little town on the edge of the desert, an outlaw could buy a jug of moonshine and enjoy it in relative peace and security. It was the era of

Main canyon, Robbers Roost

prohibition, and most saloons in the bigger towns served only soda pop to strangers.

A day or two later, after finishing his business in Green River, Ephraim rode to Hanksville to meet up with his drunken partners and escort them back to the safety of the Robbers Roost. His packsaddles were loaded with food and supplies.

———————

All too soon, it seemed, it was time to do something about the cattle Bill had left over on the Big Flat. It was too risky for Bill to go there himself, so Ephraim offered to gather his steers for him. The men talked it over as they ate their evening meal in the mouth of a shallow cave, somewhere in the Robbers Roost.

"It's purdy late in the season, but I'll go over there and gather all I can," Eph was saying as he huddled next to the campfire with a tin plate of beans and biscuits balanced in his lap. "You boys better stay on this side of the river. You got a few hundred head of cows over there, but probably less than a hundred and twenty steers. I think me and Kenny can handle it. We'll push 'em up Dubinky Wash and take 'em to the rail yard at Thompson."

"I sure hate to have you do the job alone," Bill said, from the flickering shadows on the opposite side of the fire.

"It's okay," Eph assured him. "I sure appreciate your help on this side of the river. Laterite and the White Rim are bigger country than the Big Flat and it would have taken me all winter to gather my steers alone. And besides, the Big Flat is closer to Moab and I can get home without swimmin' the river. That's important to an old buck like me when the weather gets cold like this."

Ephraim continued.

"While I'm there, do you want me to push the rest of your cows off the Big Flat and put 'em down on the White Rim and along the river bottoms with my stock? I think there's enough grass this winter to get 'em through all right. Maybe we can take another look at things when it warms up in the spring. What do ya say?"

"No, by Gawd" Bill growled from across the fire. "You leave my cows and young heifers over there. I want old Albert Beach and John Jackson to see my brand once in a while. I'm not lettin' those buzzards run me off that range. I told 'em I was there to stay, and by damn, I'm there to stay. Especially after all the lyin' they did to put me and Tom in jail."

Ephraim didn't answer for a while. He just sat and looked into the fire. Finally, he raised his eyes to look at Bill, and he said very quietly, "I'll do what you want me to do, Bill. We're partners in this business and I promised to help you out. But damn it, it'll be the death of you if you keep fightin' with those men. If you get your cows off 'a there this whole thing just might blow over."

"You leave my cows and heifer calves over there," Bill said, forcefully. "My stock will still be there when the rest of those outfits are gone. Nobody is gonna run me off that range."

Ephraim put his empty plate down on a big rock. He then sat back with his hands behind his head and looked up at the stars. A juniper limb in the fire popped and crackled, sprinkling sparks like tiny fireflies in the cool, night air. Finally he spoke, "I'll leave in the morning and go over there and see what I can do. You boys better stay here and lay low. I'll try to get back in six or eight weeks with supplies. Can you hang tough until them?"

"We'll be all right," Bill assured him. "There's lots of deer on these cedar ridges. If things get too bad we can sneak back into Hanksville and buy a few things. Those people were purdy decent to us over there."

———— • ✦ •– ————

Ten days later, the sun was dropping low toward the west. Afternoon shadows filled the slickrock canyons on the San Rafael Reef and patches of old snow glistened on the shady side of the pinyons. Bill and Tom were skinning a deer near the mouth of their cave when a horse and rider came into the camp. The outlaws were caught flat-footed. They didn't see or hear him coming until he was right on top of them. Lucky for them, it was Uncle Ephraim.

Normally, ol' Ephraim would have teased and made sarcastic remarks about how he got the drop on the unsuspecting fugitives, but this time he didn't say anything. He just tied his horse to a pinyon tree, loosened the cinch, and went to the fire to warm himself. The boys could tell that something was bad wrong.

"What's going on, Eph? You've only been gone a week or so. What's happened?"

Eph looked at the two young men for a while without speaking. His eyes were sad, but somehow fearful, too. Finally, he spoke.

"Most of your cows are dead, Bill. I found 'em scattered all over the range. Looks like somebody's been shootin' 'em."

A stunned silence fell over the camp. Then Bill spoke from deep down in his guts, his voice trembling with rage, "I'll kill those sons-a-bitches!"

"Now, Bill," Ephraim said impatiently, reaching out to touch the younger man on the shoulder. "We don't know who did it. It could have been anybody."

"It had to be John Jackson and old man Beach," Bill growled.

"Not necessarily," Eph quickly reminded. "There's six cattle outfits on that range and it could have been any one of them. The Murphys, Taylors, Pattersons, and the Snyder-Riordan bunch are all up there, too, and they were all mad when we moved in on them."

"Hell, it might have been all of them together," Tom Perkins growled.

"That's right," Eph agreed. "It might have been all of them together. We just don't know."

"So, what did you do when you found them dead?" Bill asked, still shaking with rage.

"There wasn't much I could do," Eph confessed. "I did gather everything I could find and pushed them down to the river bottom to get them out of there. You've still got a hundred head or more, but there wasn't enough steers I could find to bother taking to Thompson. I just pushed everything off the top and put 'em down along the river. We'll sort the steers out later. There's probably still a few left up on the Big Flat somewhere. I didn't have time to look everywhere."

"Did you contact the sheriff?" Tom asked, hopefully.

"Not yet," Eph admitted. "I though I'd better get over here and give you boys the news. Maybe you can help scatter what I pushed off the top before they run out of feed in Anderson Bottom."

"Hell, it wouldn't do no good to talk to the sheriff," Bill spat. "He's one of the Murphys. He'd just send ol' Deputy Beach to investigate, and we all know how that would turn out."

"Well, like it or not, the law is about the only chance we got to make things right," Ephraim argued. "We don't know who did it for sure, and you can't just go over there and pick a fight with all of those men. There's still a warrant for your arrest and a bounty on your head. And besides, when I show the sheriff what they did to your cows up there, it's sure to help your case in court. When the judge can see they shot your cows he'll be more apt to believe they framed you for cattle rustlin' last summer."

"It doesn't matter, cause I'm not goin' back to jail," Bill said forcefully. "Nobody is gonna lock me in a cage again, ever."

"Don't be too quick to say that," Ephraim argued. "You might have to surrender to clear your name. You boys can't just hide out here on the desert forever. Sooner or later you gotta go back to town to face the charges and get this mess cleaned up."

"I'll make a mess of old John Jackson's face if he ever crosses my path again," Bill promised. "I knocked the shit out of his pups and I can take the old dog, too."

"Now, Bill," Eph said quickly. "You boys are in enough trouble already. You just scatter those cows along the river bottom there and I'll ride back into Moab and file a complaint with the sheriff. You fellers take the law into your own hands and you just might end up gettin' yourselves killed. Your mothers wouldn't like that much. You boys let me take care of it in town. Maybe I can work something out with the sheriff so you don't have to go back to jail."

The next morning the men split up. Eph said he couldn't take another cold river crossing so he was going to ride thirty miles to the town of Green River and cross the river on the bridge. Bill and Tom saddled up and headed for Anderson Bottom to scatter what was left of Bill's cows. As they left their Robbers Roost hideout, the sky was dark and gloomy. A big storm was on the way.

As they rode along, Bill asked Tom if he would scatter the cows along the river by himself. Bill said he was going to ride up on the Big Flat and look things over for himself. He said it would be better if he went alone. The two of them might attract attention.

"I know Uncle Eph wouldn't lie to me," Bill said. "But I gotta see it with my own eyes. If it's really as bad as Eph says it is, I gotta do somethin' about it. It's free range up there on the Big Flat and I just can't let those guys do this to me."

"Don't go gettin' yourself killed," Tom admonished. "You're still a wanted man and they might shoot you if they see you up there nosin' around."

"I can take care of myself," Bill promised.

"So what you gonna do when you find your cows all full of bullet holes up there?" Tom asked cautiously.

"If they've been shootin' my cows they've declared war," Bill said. "And they don't know yet who they're messin' with. Old man Beach told me once that there's more than one way to skin a cat, and he's about to find out I'm a cat-skinnin' fool."

"You be careful, Bill. All the cows in the world ain't worth gettin' killed over."

<hr>

Bill did find his cows dead. Dozens and dozens of them. The rotting carcasses were scattered all over the Big Flat. By close examination, he found bullet holes in some of the remains and empty bullet casings on the ground near some of the others. On several of the dead cows his T-4 brand was still clearly visible, stretched tight on a partially mummified cowhide. That proud mark of his ownership seemed to scream to the heavens for justice.

A phantom rode the Big Flat country for the next several weeks. No one ever saw the phantom, but he was there, and he was busy. Cows started coming up missing. Whole herds of cows simply disappeared, and the losses were indiscriminate. All of the ranchers on the Big Flat lost livestock. Some of them lost a lot of livestock.

It was mid-winter, December and January, when the losses occurred, a time of cold weather when most cowmen were huddled in a cabin with a warm fire and a hot coffeepot. The ranchers didn't notice their cows were disappearing for a few weeks.

When the losses were discovered and the alarm sounded, the ranchers found hundreds of cow tracks going down the Horsethief Trail to the river. There, the tracks went into the icy water and simply disappeared. Just below where the cows had entered the water, the river entered a narrow canyon with near-vertical sandstone walls. For a few miles there was no place the swimming bovines could leave the water without a desperate struggle. A few days later came reports of dozens of dead cows washed up on sandbars near the Glen Canyon settlement of Hite.

The ranchers didn't all respond in the same way. Some started to gather their stock immediately to move them off the Big Flat and save what they could. Others loaded their Winchesters and began a deadly manhunt. All of them called in their relatives, friends, and hired hands to bunch and sort the cows that were left. Armed guards were posted and the whole country was up in arms.

But more cattle disappeared. For a few more weeks, small bunches of cows that had escaped the general roundup kept coming up missing. Tracks of a single horse and rider were found where the cows had gone over the rim and off the ledges.

Cowboys with guns hunted the phantom day and night. By day, they scoured the rims and followed horse tracks for miles through the junipers and sage. In the moonlight they rode to the tops of the hills to look for the flicker of an outlaw campfire. They never could find one. Still the phantom came like the wind, from out of nowhere, and then he was gone.

When the ranchers bunched their cattle for protection, they quickly began to run out of feed. Many hundreds of cattle were trailed off the Big Flat and taken to the lower country closer to Moab. Most were crowded onto already overstocked ranges, much to the anger and frustrations of other ranchers already running stock there. Some of the cattle were taken to pastures close to town where they could be fed with a pitchfork and properly protected. Many were eventually sold to save them from starving.

By early spring, the Big Flat country was empty. The March wind moaned over the bleached and broken bones of the Moab cattle industry.

Outlaw Cave on the Robbers Roost used by Bill Tibbetts and Tom Perkins in 1924

CHAPTER 16

VANISHING INTO THE MIST

THE FIRST BLUSH OF SPRING BROUGHT NEW colors of life to the Robbers Roost country. A bright sun warmed the yellow sand and the cactus and sage began to blossom. The red rocks and blue sky became clean and bright again. Even the pinyon and juniper trees stood taller and greener as they reached for the welcoming sun with open arms. The cold, miserable winter was finally over.

The last of the Robbers Roost outlaws welcomed the warmer weather, but they knew they were entering a new and dangerous time. The ranchers over on the Big Flat were stirred up like a nest of hornets, and with green grass and longer days, the lawmen would soon be out in force. The boys knew they would be hunted like rabid wolves. They cleaned their guns and kept a sharp eye out.

They spotted the rider coming from a few miles away. The man was alone and he stayed out in the open where he could easily be seen. It was obvious that he wanted the outlaws to spot him, and they were quickly convinced that it had to be Uncle Ephraim. They were right.

As the horseman came along the top of a ridge, trying to skyline himself to be better seen, the outlaws stepped out from behind some rocks. Each had a bandana tied around his nose and mouth and they had guns in their hands.

"Halt! Who goes there?" Bill challenged, delighted to have gotten the drop on the older man this time.

Eph pulled up his horse and rolled his eyes impatiently. The boys laughed and pulled off their robber's masks.

Then Eph said, very sarcastically, "It's about time. I nearly rode this horse to death tryin' to get yer attention. I was beginnin' to think you boys might have left the country. Didn't look like you'd been at the old cave for quite some time."

"Yeah, we moved to a new location a month or so ago," Bill said as he holstered his .44 and reached out to shake his uncle's hand. "Our new cave is a little more secluded."

"Well, take me to your new camp," Eph said eagerly. "I'm still damp from crossin' the river and damn near froze to death."

At the new outlaw camp, Eph thawed out by the fire and then he got down to business. "What the hell you boys been up to? I been hearin' some awful rumors around town."

"What ya been hearin'?" Bill asked with a wicked smile.

"I've heard the big outfits have been losing a whole lot of stock," Eph said with an anxious brow. "I've heard they've been findin' dead cows floatin' down the river. I've heard they've been findin' cattle stranded on sandbars ten miles down the canyon. They say all the cows on the Big Flat have been mixed up and scattered from the Island all the way to the Book Cliffs. They tell me they been findin' cows boxed-in under the ledges."

"Was you the guy who did all of that, Bill?"

"It was purdy cold up there on the Big Flat and I thought some of those cows might like to go to sunny California," Bill grinned.

"Well, I guess you got even, all right, but you sure messed up your chances for gettin' the law on your side."

"To hell with them," Bill growled. "The law's never been on my side, anyway."

"It's too bad you feel that way," Eph said, rather sadly. "Cause I've been tryin' to negotiate a surrender so you boys could get this mess all cleaned up. But now you got no chance. They're gonna come for you this summer, and they've been talkin' about hirin' one of those airplanes."

For a while they all stood around the fire in silence as the full weight of what Eph had just said soaked into their personal reality. They could hide from the sheriff and run from a posse, but they couldn't evade eyes in the sky. The prospects for their future were suddenly very grim.

"How're they tellin' the story in the newspaper?" Tom Perkins asked, trying to lighten things up a bit. "Is ol' Deputy Beach still a hero?"

"They haven't had a word about it in the newspaper," Eph informed him. "And that's what's scary about this. Everything I've heard I got from the pool hall and the barbershop. I think they're keepin' it out of the paper because it's got real personal now. I think they're plannin' to kill you boys."

———•◦•———

Later that night, the fugitives sat around the campfire enjoying some of the coffee and sugar Eph had brought in his saddlebags. A big moon moved silently across the sky and silver shadows rippled over the ledges and through the trees. Far off down the ridge a coyote yipped impatiently, the sound echoing in the canyons.

"Do ya really think they'll bring an airplane?"

"I think they'll do it," came the answer from Uncle Eph. "And I wouldn't be surprised if they don't get some help from the governor. Some of those guys donate political money to buy the ear and sympathies of heavyweight politicians. I'm sure they're callin' in their markers already. They might have some state and federal marshals here in a few weeks. If I were you boys, I'd get

{ 124 }

the hell outta here while you still can."

"Yeah, I guess you're right," Bill conceded. "This thing's gotten way out of hand."

For a while, no one spoke. The fire popped and crackled. The distant coyote moaned like the wind in the ledges.

"Even if they don't kill you, you might end up spending fifteen or twenty years in the state pen." Eph said. "They know you pushed those cows in the river and they won't let you get away with it. It doesn't matter anymore what they did. They've got the law ridin' with them, and probably the governor, too."

———————

Over the next few days, they were able to make a deal. Bill signed over his T-4 brand and all of his cattle to Uncle Eph. Ephraim gave Bill all of the money he had with him at the time and promised to pay a fair market price for Bill's cows once he was able to figure out how many were left. He would deposit the money in a joint account in the Moab bank. It would be there for Bill when he could get back to claim it. Eph promised to take care of Bill's mother's cows and pasture old Ute until Bill could come back for him.

A few days later, in the middle of the night, a couple of hobos snuck aboard an empty boxcar at the railroad siding in Thompson Springs. The train had stopped to take on water and coal. She was pointed toward Colorado. Ephraim stood near the railcar holding the reins of three horses as he told the boys goodbye. Bill reached out and patted old Ute on the cheek and told him to be a good horse until he got back.

Then the train whistle squealed and great billows of steam and smoke belched out over the nighttime prairie as connectors popped and big wheels squeaked and started to turn. A long, rolling tremor rattled down the length of the train as the engine huffed and puffed and started to move, grinding iron wheels on cold iron rails.

"You boys take care of yourselves," Ephraim called as the boxcar began to move away.

"Kiss my mother for me," Bill called back.

"You kiss my ass," Ephraim hollered above the noise of the puffing engine.

The outlaws and Uncle Ephraim were all laughing as the train pulled away. Eph stood holding the horses until the train was well down the track. He then stepped up into the saddle and turned the horses toward the desert. He had to hide the extra saddles before the sheriff figured things out.

———————

The boys made their way to Kansas. There they got work on a big farm. The farmer told them he was hiring full-time farmhands, and they soon found out what full-time employment meant to a Kansas farmer. The only time they had off was when they were eating or sleeping. The farmer kept them busy for twelve to fourteen hours a day, seven days a week.

It didn't take long to get all of the Kansas farming they wanted, and the fugitives migrated to Oklahoma. There they ended up picking cotton and doing farm work again near the little town of Watonga in the west central part of the state. There were a lot of cowboys in Oklahoma, and amateur rodeos were popular events. By competing in the rodeos, Bill was able to supplement his income, and because of his skill and daring, he became a local celebrity known as "Cowboy Jim Lee." Jim Lee was the alias he used while hiding from the law.

In Oklahoma, Bill met a young woman who changed everything. She was a pretty girl, the daughter of a shopkeeper. Her father owned the Agens Mercantile in Watonga. Jewel Agens worked with her father and she was the main attraction in town for many of the young men of the area. There were always a few moonstruck young fellows hanging around the store like stray cats.

Cowboy Jim Lee was different. He was cool, confident, and infinitely more mature than the stray cats. And he was a rodeo star, a true American hero. The Agens Mercantile had some old posters of Buffalo Bill's Wild West Show hanging on the wall, and Cowboy Jim Lee looked and acted like he had just stepped out of the poster. He was handsome, tough, and he always dressed the part.

The young cowboy stopped by the store often and he was a careful shopper. He always talked with Jewel for a few minutes before deciding on his purchase. Jewel was a good sales lady and she sold him all kinds of goods, even things he didn't really need. They would talk, Jewel would giggle, and sometimes the young cowboy would blush. They got to know each other very

Jewel, first wedding in Oklahoma

well. Bill was polite but evasive when she tried to pin him down about his family and his origins.

Bill had always been something of a lady's man with his rugged good looks and manly manners, and the Oklahoma prairie flower was charmed by the attentions of the rough and tumble cowboy with the mysterious past. Betty Jewel Agens married Cowboy Jim Lee in 1926. He was 28 and she was 23.

Jewel was a good wife for Bill. She loved the man and always stood by him. She held his trust, his love, and the secrets of his heart as her treasures. She was also strong, healthy, and full of life, the kind of woman who could follow him anywhere.

As for Bill, he was completely devoted to Jewel. In her he found the love, compassion, and strong bond of family togetherness that was denied him during his troubled childhood. In her loving care, the wild man of the desert became a devoted husband, father, and grandfather. Jewel, the prairie flower, could tame him.

For most of two years the newlyweds lived in Watonga. Then, in 1928, Bill, Jewel, and Tom Perkins moved to New Mexico. Bill was looking for better opportunities to provide for his family. Working on other people's farms and riding in rodeos didn't promise much of a future for a family man who had just turned 30. The family was growing, too. His son, William Robert, had been born in 1927 and Jewel would soon have another baby.

They lived in Santa Fe and the men made their living breaking horses for the New Mexico State Police. Bill was confident, competent, and outgoing, and he got along well with the state troopers. No one suspected he was a fugitive from justice. As a state employee and New Mexico's top horse wrangler, the cowboy Jim Lee became good friends with New Mexico's governor, Richard C. Dillon. But times were changing and the police were buying more and more automobiles and fewer and fewer horses. Soon, the boys had to find work elsewhere.

Bill and Tom found jobs with the San Busco Lumber Company in Santa Fe. They saved their money, and in a short time they were able to make down payments on ranches of their own. As Jim Lee, Bill bought an old Spanish ranch called The Tarrion. He subdivided the land and made a handsome profit.

Tom Perkins bought some old Spanish ranch property, too, and soon had some good luck and some bad luck. Tom found a small iron pot full of Spanish gold coins buried in the walls of an old adobe building he was tearing down. But when he took his glittering good fortune to town to show his friends, the State of New Mexico confiscated his find. He was told there was a law on the books that buried Spanish treasure belonged to the state.

In 1930, Bill's mother received a letter from a Mr. James Lee. The letter was postmarked Santa Fe, New Mexico. Inside she found the first news of her wayward son in over five years. He told her he was married, a father, in good health, and doing well in his new surroundings. He invited her to visit sunny New Mexico to meet his bride and two young sons.

Amy was delighted to hear from her oldest boy. She had almost given up hope of ever hearing from him again. Amy and Uncle Ephraim made the journey to Santa Fe where they enjoyed a long overdue reunion.

———— ·•·•· ————

"It's sure good to see you, Bill." Ephraim said as he sat in the shade of the grape vines on the veranda. I'm happy to see you've done so good. I was worried about you and Tom, never knowin' how things turned out and all."

"Yeah, we've both done good," Bill smiled proudly.

"Have another glass of lemonade," Bill said, as he opened another bottle of beer.

"So tell me, Eph, did the sheriff ever send that airplane out on the Roost to find me and Tom?"

"He did," Eph responded. "That airplane buzzed around out there for most of a week. They flew right over me two or three times, scared the hell out of old Sugarfoot. Funny thing, though, nothin' was ever in the newspaper about it."

"I guess we got out of there just in time," Bill said soberly.

"Are you figurin' to move back to Moab one of these days?"

"Can't for another couple of years," Bill explained. "The way I understand it, the statute of limitations runs out after seven years. The warrant for my jailbreak and trouble with the sheriff was issued in September 1924. I better not show my face up there till at least 1932. That'll give the warrant a few extra months to run out."

"Hell, I think they've quit lookin' for you." Eph said.

"Oh, I don't know. Old man Beach and John Jackson are probably still on the prod. I don't think those two old buzzards will give up that easy."

"Beach doesn't live in Moab anymore," Ephraim said. "He sold out not long after you and Tom went to Kansas. I don't know where he ended up, Arizona, maybe."

"I'll be damned," Bill shrugged. "I didn't know about that. What's old John Jackson doin'?"

"He's still runnin' a few cows over on Ten Mile," Eph smiled. "He pulled all of his stock off the Big Flat after you gave most of 'em a bath. He was half the summer that year gatherin' up stragglers down along the river there. It was a hell of a mess. We still find a lonesome old cow down there once in a while still wearin' his brand."

Bill laughed out loud. "Serves him right," he said as he clapped his hands with delight.

"Jackson is makin' most of his livin' nowadays as a moneylender," Eph said.

"You mean a banker?"

"No, a moneylender, like they used to have in the old days. For a little collateral and ten percent interest, he'll lend money to almost anyone."

"You don't say," Bill mused.

"What happened to the rest of the cowmen over on the Big Flat?"

"Taylors quit and sold out," Eph said. "Patterson moved everything down to Lisbon Valley in San Juan County. The Snyder-Riordan outfit pulled out and went to Colorado. The Murphys are still hangin' on, but the outfit ain't nothin' like it used to be. I don't think they'll make another year."

"And how are you and Mother doin' in the cattle business?"

"Aw, darn it, Bill. I didn't want to talk about that yet."

"Why not?" Bill asked with an anxious brow. He pulled his chair a little closer to the older man and asked again. "Why not, Eph?"

"Well, I hope you're not mad, but I sold out last year," Eph said as he fidgeted with his shirt collar and loosened his necktie just a touch. "I sold the whole shebang. All my cows and all the rights to my rangeland. Sold out to a guy named Art Murry. He moved the whole show up on the Big Flat."

"What about Mother's cows?"

"She sold out, too, Bill. She's still got a few, but Kenny is takin' care of 'em now. He's got her stock and his' up on the Big Flat."

"Kenny is just a kid."

"Yeah, but he's a damn good cowboy. If he keeps goin' he'll own five hundred head by the time he's twenty."

"So why did you quit, Eph?"

"I'm 51 years old, Bill. That's half a century. I got gout and arthritis. I just couldn't take crossin' that darn river no more. When I sleep on the ground I get so damn stove-up it's noon before I can get in the saddle. I'm afraid one of these days one of those old wrangs is gonna buck me off and nobody will ever find my bones out there on that desert. It was just time to quit, Bill."

"Whatever happened to the money you was goin' to pay me for my stock?" Bill asked.

"I got it with me," Ephraim smiled. "A few thousand dollars and change. It's been in the bank in Moab since you left town."

The men were interrupted when the women came from inside of the house. Jewel walked over and put her arms around Bill's neck. She leaned forward, kissed him on the forehead, and said, "Your mother has been telling me all about your life, Bill."

"Aw, I already told you most of that stuff."

"You did," Jewel purred, "but you sure left out a lot."

"What can I say?" Bill blushed, giving his mother a scolding look.

"We've got to do something before your mother goes back home," Jewel said.

"What's that?"

"We've got to get married."

"We already are married."

"I married a man named Jim Lee," Jewel said with a sweet but menacing tone. "I'd rather be married to Bill Tibbetts."

"Well, maybe we can get your minister to…."

"Absolutely not." Jewel interrupted. "We got married in a Baptist church last time. I'm not going down there with two little kids and tell the minister I want to get married. You're going to find a justice of the peace somewhere who doesn't know either one of us."

"Oh, all right," Bill grinned.

Ephraim got up and walked away to keep from laughing.

Two days later, Mrs. Jim Lee became Mrs. Bill Tibbetts. Bill's mother was the maid of honor and Uncle Ephraim the best man.

Jewel loved her role as a wife and mother. She doted over her husband and family, and she was a very busy young homemaker. Her four sons were born in the space of six years: William Robert in 1927, Jimmy Willard in 1929, Rodney Gail in 1930, and Raymond Moore in 1932.

Bill and Jewel

CHAPTER 17

THE HOMECOMING

THE 1930S BROUGHT THE GREAT DEPRESSION, the Dust Bowl in the Midwest, the end of Prohibition, and the statute of limitations for Bill Tibbetts and Tom Perkins. For seven years the boys had lived as fugitives, exiled to the nether regions of the great American Southwest. But now they could go home again without worrying too much about the long arm of the law. There was also a new sheriff in town, a man who didn't remember the transgressions of the brash young cowboys back in 1924.

Bill Tibbetts, Jewel, and their four young sons, came home to Moab with all of their belongings piled high on a flatbed truck. This time, Tom Perkins had opted to stay in New Mexico. Tom had converted his ranching property to a dude ranch and he was doing well in spite of the Depression. He never did return to the land of Moab to live.

By the 1930s, the social center of Moab had moved from the pool hall to the Moab Garage. Everyone who was anyone spent an hour or two at the garage during the day. It was the place to go to find out about the news, what was happening around the world, and who was doing what to whom in town. A big coffee pot was at the center of the action.

It was a beautiful summer morning when Moab's prodigal son walked into the Moab Garage. His old nemesis, John Jackson, the moneylender and former big-time stockman, was entertaining the coffee crowd with a long and humorous story. Jackson stopped short when he saw Bill walk through the door. His face flushed red and his eyes flashed with lightning as he said, right out loud, "That Goddamn horse thief is back in town!"

Bill knocked the man into a large glass display case, shattering glass and scattering fan belts and oilcans all over the floor. Coffee spilled and dust flew. Chairs tipped over and morning newspapers littered the floor. Jackson was in his mid-fifties, but he was no slouch when it came to fighting. He gave back about as good as he got. The men went through a plate glass window and landed in the street in a shower of glass, curses, and flailing fists. Bill finally ending up with two men holding each arm to restrain him. Jackson was bruised and bloodied, but his ego was hurt more than his jaw. He was a big man and he had always been the top dog in town.

After Jackson went home to change his soiled shirt and get some ice for his swollen lip, Bill went back in the garage and offered to pay for the damages. One of the owners told him there would be no charge. "Anyone who can do that to John Jackson doesn't have to pay for the mess," the man said with a big smile. "This one's on us."

———•-•-•———

Just a day or two later, Bill Tibbetts knocked on John Jackson's front door. Jackson came to the door with his hackles and his dukes up, ready for combat.

"I hear you got money to lend," Bill said with an impish grin.

Jackson just stood there with his fists up, glaring at Bill.

"I need a loan to get back in the stock business. You got money to lend?"

"Why the hell would I lend you money?" Jackson hissed.

"Cause I hate banks and bankers and I hear you're an honest man," Bill said with a wry smile. "Besides, you got a hell of a good left hook." Bill reached up and touched the big purple bruise on his cheek and smiled. Jackson noticed for the first time that Bill's eye was black.

Jackson smiled just a little. "You don't do so bad yourself," he said. And then he licked his split and swollen lip with the tip of his tongue.

"I think between the two of us, we could take the whole town," Bill grinned. "What do you think?"

"I think so, too," Jackson agreed, putting his fists down and relaxing his shoulders just a little.

"So why don't we put all of this behind us?" Bill offered. "I'm movin' back to town and I don't want to fight with you every time we meet on the street. I'm willin' to hang up my spurs on this whole deal if you'll meet me halfway."

"You got a lot of guts to be sayin' that," Jackson growled. "You scattered my cows for twenty miles down that river and you drowned a hell of a bunch of 'em."

"And you shot and killed mine," Bill said with his chin up and storm clouds in his eyes.

For a time neither man spoke. They just stood and looked at each other, posturing like fighting roosters. They stood eye-to-eye and toe-to-toe, but their minds were back on the Big Flat and the river bottoms of seven and eight years ago. It took a few minutes for all of that water to run under the bridge.

Finally, Jackson dropped his eyes and said okay. "I'm willin' to have a truce, Bill. No sense in draggin' this out for another ten years. I'm getting too old to fistfight about it and the sheriff will lock me up if I shoot your sorry ass. We might as well be friends."

Bill held out his open right hand. "Shake on it," he offered.

Jackson took Bill's hand in an iron grip. "Done," he said.

"Okay, now that we're friends, I need to talk to you about a loan," Bill grinned. "I was serious about that."

{ 132 }

"By Gawd, you got more balls than any man I ever knew," Jackson said, shaking his head in disbelief.

"I'm an honest man," Bill said. "Just like you."

Jackson rolled his eyes with longsuffering resignation. Then he took a deep breath and stepped back inside the house. Holding the door open, he said, with just a touch of sarcasm, "Come in the house, friend. Let's talk about it." Over the next few years, what began as a truce and mutual respect for each other's strength and willingness to fight developed into a genuine friendship.

———•••———

With the money he borrowed from Jackson, Bill got a start in the sheep business. With his mother, Amy, he bought a herd of sheep and moved them to Island in the Sky. He filed for a homestead on Grays Pasture and built a small, one-room log cabin there. Bill, Jewel, their four little boys, and Bill's mother lived in the cabin for a time and tended the sheep. Ephraim joined them in the venture and filed for a homestead of his own near Whitbeck Rock on the Big Flat.

It didn't take long for conflicts to develop between the sheepherders and the cowboy who grazed the Big Flat. Sheep and cows never fit well together on the same patch of ground. And then, too, Ephraim had sold his cows and grazing rights to Art Murry in 1929, and Murry was not happy about sharing grass with the Tibbetts, Moore, and Allred sheep outfit. He saw it as the violation of a contract, even though Ephraim was the only one who had signed an agreement with him.

As the conflict with the neighbor deepened, Bill decided that sheepherding was not a great way to make a living. Wool prices were down, sheep required much more attention than cattle, and things were primitive and crowded in the little log cabin. The women were a long ways from town and two cooks can spoil the stew. In just a short time, Bill sold out, forfeited his homestead claim, and moved back to New Mexico. In Santa Fe, he opened a real estate office and went back to work for the San Busco Lumber Company.

But he just couldn't stay in New Mexico. Like his mother, his heart was on the Utah desert. In the late 1930s, Bill moved back to Moab and decided to go back into the cow business. He moved his family to Hanksville in 1938 and tried to start a ranch on the south end of the Henry Mountains near Star Springs. His ranching venture failed because Star Springs was very remote, the Taylor Grazing Act was changing the face of livestock production in the West, and Bill didn't feel that his family was being well treated by the people of Hanksville while he was away. Jewel was a Baptist and not easily assimilated into the deeply-rooted Mormon culture of the little town. After three years of giving it a good try, Bill moved his family back to Moab in 1941.

In Moab, Bill tried farming for a while, and then he went back to selling real estate. He was a good realtor and made a decent living. He also worked as a city marshal and then served as a deputy sheriff for Grand County. He was a good lawman, fair, honest, and without pretension.

In early 1945, while serving as a lawman, Bill was tipped off that a group of local ruffians was planning a raid on a nearby prisoner of war camp at Dalton Wells, a few miles north of Moab.

Word had recently been received that a couple of men from Moab had been killed in the war, and a few angry hotheads were out for revenge.

As the drunken mob approached the POW camp, Bill was there with Claron Bailey and Ralph Miller to intercept them. Though badly outnumbered and heavily outgunned, Bill was able to talk the men out of doing any harm. A man less respected, with less courage and less conviction, might not have been able to do it. After listening to Bill for only a short time, the mobsters went back to Moab to drown their sorrows in whiskey instead of blood.

Jewel got sick in the late 1940s and almost died. She had major surgery and the doctors thought they had lost her for a while. But she came back stronger than ever. Jewel was physically weak for a time, but something happened to her during her near-death experience that made her more spiritual. Those close to her considered her psychic. She amazed her family several times with predictions that came true.

The doctors told Jewel that she had to walk to regain her strength. So she began walking every day. She didn't like walking through town with all of the dogs, traffic, and neighbors, so Bill began taking her out on the desert to do her walking. He began to walk with her, and together they hiked many hundreds of miles. As they walked, they picked up pretty rocks and fossils and soon it became an obsession with them. They became avid rockhounds. Jewel grew strong with her daily hikes in the desert and soon she was restored to full health.

In 1959, Bill and Jewel bought the Horsethief Ranch. It was a special place for Bill, since he and Kenny Allred had been the first cowboys to discover the lower spring there, back in 1924. It was special, too, because they purchased the place from Kenny Allred who had bought the property from Art Murry in 1951. Bill and Jewel lived at the ranch for six years, tending a few cows while gathering one of the most impressive rock collections in southeastern Utah.

It was a great time for them. They were semi-isolated in the beautiful country they loved and they truly enjoyed each other's company. In 1965, shortly after the creation of nearby Canyonlands National Park, they sold the ranch to Mac and Alice McKinney and moved back to Moab.

Then suddenly, their lives ended. On August 9, 1969, Bill and Jewel Tibbetts were killed by a drunk driver on the highway south of Moab. They died together, side by side, the way they had lived for 43 years.

———— • ————

Ephraim Moore remained firmly rooted in that earlier time when the world was simple and the pace of living was slow. He did his farming and traveling with horses and wagons into the late 1940s. In his later years he kept a few sheep and cows and farmed the old Moore homestead in Moab. True to his church and religious principles to the end of his days, he died in Moab in 1950.

Tom Perkins never returned to Moab to live. He stayed in Santa Fe for many years and then sold his ranch and moved to Salt Lake City. Genealogy records are scant, but they suggest that he never married. Tom died in 1951 at the age of 62.

Eph Moore on his farm in Moab Valley, 1940s

Kenny Allred married and raised a large family. Always a cowboy at heart, he carried the Moore, Tibbetts, and Allred ranching tradition into the late 1950s, and then he sold out and bought an apartment house. In the early 1960s, he went to work for Atlas Minerals Corporation at the uranium mill near Moab. He died in 1998 at the age of 83.

"Peg Leg" Will Moore died in 1945, one of the last of the old-time cowboys. Never owning a ranch of his own, he rode for other men and other brands until the end of the trail. Like his younger brother Ephraim, he remained a committed bachelor his whole life.

Amy Moore Tibbetts Allred died in 1948. Her body was buried in Moab but the longings of her heart lived on. In the end she looked forward to a grand reunion with her cowboy sweetheart. She hoped to meet him in the land beyond the sunset where the red rocks touch the sky. If God allows homesteads in heaven, they are building a fine ranch there, with a beautiful home, someplace where a cold spring of water bubbles up from the oak brush in the shadow of a long, pine ridge.

And so closed a final chapter in the saga of the Old West. They were members of that last generation to remember the pioneer times and a world without automobiles, telephones and airplanes. They were tough and self-reliant people, flawed in many ways, but true to the values and principles that founded our nation - men who honored chivalry and women who cherished virtue.

Some of us remember, and we miss them.

Tibbetts Arch in the Maze

EPILOGUE

BILL TIBBETTS LEFT HIS MARK ON SOUTHEASTERN UTAH IN MANY WAYS. In the 1940s, when the Unites States Geological Survey was fixing place names for official government maps of the Canyonlands area, they sought out a few of the old-timers around Moab as consultants. It was Bill Tibbetts who gave them the old cowboy names for most of the river bottoms and prominent landmarks along the Green and Colorado rivers. Many of the canyons and topographic features within Canyonlands National Park bear the names Bill Tibbetts gave to the government mapmakers. Place names like Turks Head, Grays Pasture, Queen Anne Bottom, Cleopatra's Chair, and Candlestick Tower all came from his mind and memory. It is true that Bill was not the first to name most of those places, but it is because of him that many of the old names are on the maps today.

It is fitting that a couple of natural sandstone arches in Canyonlands National Park bear the Tibbetts name. Tibbetts Arch, or Bill Tibbetts Arch, is found in the Maze District not far from Elaterite Basin where Bill and Ephraim Moore ran cattle in the 1920s. Even today, the arch is in a very remote and seldom visited region, accessible only by four-wheel-drive vehicles. The country looks much the same as when Bill and Ephraim first went there in 1919. Bill would be happy about that.

Jewel Tibbetts Arch, named for Bill's wife, is in the Island in the Sky District, accessible by a short hike. Both Tibbetts arches are listed on Park Service maps.

For many years, Bill's sons believed their father had never left his name anywhere but in the secret cave in Arches National Park. But in 1988, an employee of the National Park Service, Gary Cox, found Bill's name carved on the roof of a shallow cave near the rim of Horseshoe (Barrier) Canyon on the Robbers Roost. The date of the inscription is September 15, 1924, six weeks after Bill and Tom Perkins broke out of jail in Moab. The cave must have served as their first hideout after their harrowing escape to the Green River bottoms and Elaterite Basin. As far as anyone knows today, that single inscription is the only testament of Bill Tibbetts, in his own hand, to be found anywhere on the rocks of the canyon country and the Robbers Roost.

Ray Tibbetts at homestead site in 1980

ACKNOWLEDGEMENTS

RAYMOND MOORE TIBBETTS OF MOAB, UTAH, HAS BEEN THE DRIVING FORCE BEHIND THIS BOOK. Ray is the youngest son of James William (Bill) Tibbetts, Jr., the principal character of this story. Ray recognized many years ago that his father had lived a remarkable life, and by recording his story, an important account of the early history of Moab and Grand County, Utah, might be preserved. He also knew the story would make an interesting and entertaining book.

In 1989, Ray and his daughter, Cynthia Tibbetts Lyman, along with Jean Akens, wrote a brief, unpublished account of this story entitled, Island in the Sky: The Life and Times of Bill Tibbetts. An edited version of that story was printed in Canyon Legacy magazine in 1992.

Ray also contributed information for a chapter in the book, HorseThief Ranch: An Oral History, written and published by Michael Behrendt in 1985.

The author of this book has drawn heavily from those sources, as well as personal interviews with Ray Tibbetts and old newspaper accounts from The Times Independent of Moab, Utah. The author has visited many of the sites described in this book, most often with Ray Tibbetts as guide, friend, and interpreter of local history.

Ray Tibbetts is a former Grand County Commissioner who was instrumental in the establishment of Canyonlands National Park in the early 1960s. As plans for the park were being developed, Ray took several high-ranking government officials, including former Secretary of the Interior Stewart Udall on helicopter tours of the canyon country to show them places that he (Ray Tibbetts) felt needed to be protected. Most of those places were included within the park boundaries.

And yet, Ray was a key player in the Sagebrush Rebellion of the 1970s and 1980s, appearing before congressional committees to protest BLM encroachment on the sovereign rights of state and local governments to manage roads and public lands within their jurisdictions. While being an advocate for conservation, parks, and monuments, he is not a fan of wilderness for the sake of wilderness.

Ray is a lifelong resident of Moab, and like his father, he is a former cowboy, lawman, successful businessman, outdoorsman, and lover of the Utah desert. His intimate knowledge of the canyon country is impressive, and his help, inspiration, and encouragement have been invaluable to the writing of this book.

Bill, Jewel Tibbetts and son at their sheep camp near Gemini Bridges in the early 1930s

PHOTO CREDITS

ABOUT THE AUTHOR

Tom McCourt is a native son of the deserts and canyons of eastern Utah. An avid outdoorsman, he has worked as a farmer, a cowboy, a surveyor, a coalminer, a social worker, a newspaper staff writer and columnist, and a tour guide. Tom has a degree in Anthropology from the University of Utah and served as an Officer and a Gentleman in the U.S. Army. He and his wife Jeannie make their home in rural Carbon County, Utah.

Other Titles by Tom McCourt

THE SPLIT SKY:
A Journey of Discovery in Utah's Nine Mile Canyon

WHITE CANYON:
Remembering the Little Town at the Bottom of Lake Powell

TO BE A SOLDIER

THE MOAB STORY: *From Cowpokes to Bike Spokes*